IN THE
Midst
OF THEE

VOLUME II

REVISED 3RD EDITION

History of the Saints

IN THE
Midst
OF THEE

VOLUME II

REVISED 3RD EDITION

GLENN RAWSON AND **DENNIS LYMAN**

Copyright © Glenn Rawson 2021
Copyright © History of the Saints 2021
Sandy, Utah
Historyofthesaints.org
All rights reserved. This material may not be reproduced for personal or commercial gain. It may be used for incidental Church use. The views expressed herein are the responsibility of the author\compiler and do not represent The Church of Jesus Christ of Latter-day Saints.
ISBN 978-1-7355962-2-8
Printed in the United States of America

Thank you to all those who have shared your stories with me over the years, who have been willing to bare your soul and share a part of you for so many to see and learn from. Thank you also to all those who have listened to, loved, and shared these stories. And lastly, thank you to all my friends and family who have been a part of this work from the beginning. Glenn

Contents

Families Are Forever 1

Love as Jesus Expressed It 3

Jedediah Morgan Grant 6

Martha And Mary 9

Ahaz's Sign 11

Haircuts and Hugs 13

Jesus the Pioneer 15

Choose Ye This Day 17

Little Dog 19

The Will of the Father 21

"A New Heart" 24

The Divine Smile 26

The Duty of Prayer 27

Typing 29

A Child's Gift 31

THE FATHERHOOD OF GOD	34
OLD FAITHFUL	36
DANIEL	38
ELIJAH AND THE WIDOW	40
DAVID AND GOLIATH	43
STALLED	46
"ARE YOU A MORMON?"	48
JOHANN'S LIFE	50
SERVE THY MOTHER	52
RUN AWAY TO JESUS	54
THE ADULTEROUS WOMAN	56
BELOVED MOTHER	58
THE PHARISEE AND THE PUBLICAN	60
THE TIRE GUY	62
THE BREAD OF LIFE	65
ONLY GOD GIVES *A*s	67

STANFORD AND ARABELLA	69
THE SWINGS	72
"ARISE AND READ THE ELEVENTH CHAPTER OF ISAIAH"	73
HALL FAMILY PRAYER	75
THE WIDOW OF NAIN	77
THE COMFORTER	79
TO WHOM SHALL WE GO?	81
MISTI'S BALLOON	83
JAIRUS	85
SAMARITAN WOMAN	87
SKIING FAITH	89
THE WEIGHT SET	91
HEZEKIAH'S TEST	93
BURIED BY THE WAYSIDE	95
THE RED FLAKE	97

Obedience Always 99

Joshua and the Spies 101

Sweet-and-Sour Rice 103

The Tree of Life 105

The Dirt on the Road 107

They That Be with Us 109

The Garbage Truck Driver 111

Abraham's Test 113

"Can You See What I Just Did to You?" 115

Powerful Contradictions 117

The Parable of the Map 120

Nebuchadnezzar's Humbling 123

Old Mustard 125

Cell Phones and Prayer 127

The Least of These 129

Pain 131

THE PRESIDENT	133
IF I LOSE MY WAY	135
A FATHER'S PRAYER	138
HE WAS GONE	140
TUMBLEWEEDS	142
THE HEARTS OF THE CHILDREN	144
THE NOBLEMAN'S SON	146
KASSIE'S SOAP	148
SAUL	150
LINCOLN'S PROPOSAL	152
ROAD TRIP	154
ABRAHAM	157
HEY DIDDLE, DIDDLE, AND TRUTH	159
A CONVERSATION ABOUT PRAYER	161
"I AM DRY"	163
JAXSON AND BLAIR	165

Nothing to Fear	167
Bartimaeus the Blind Beggar	169
Asleep at the Concert	171
Stillman Pond	173
Blizzards of Experience	175
Hannah and Samuel	177
Dates with Destiny	179
Following Porcupines	181
Honor Thy Mother	183
Gnat on My Pillow	185
"In His Presence"	187
Hezekiah and Grace	190
Grateful for Gratitude	192
Joseph's Dream	194
He Knows Your Name	196
Judging Others	198

PATIENCE AND THE SONS OF THUNDER	200
MOM AND DAD	202
WHAT MONEY CAN BUY	204
PLODDING	206
"OH, IT WAS NOTHING"	208
THE TEMPTATIONS OF JESUS	210
RUTH	212
THE POWER OF IPOD	214
THING OF NAUGHT	216
WEE GRANNY	218
WORDS MATTER	220
FOR THE NEW YEAR	222
RESURRECTION MORNING	224
JESUS AND THE PRISONERS	226
BETHLEHEM TODAY	228
"ALL HE NEEDS IS A COFFIN"	231

INDEX 235

Families Are Forever

John the Beloved said, "God is love" (1 John 4:16).

Please think about this for a minute: If God is love, then love is forever; and if love is forever, then families must be forever.

Grandpa and Grandma were serving the Lord back east when it was learned that Grandpa had cancer. The doctors gave him little hope. He grew steadily worse until finally the family was called. Katie's family was one of the first to arrive. As they entered the room, Grandpa hugged and greeted each family member. While they waited for the rest of the family to show up, Katie and her sister, Annie, sat down on the floor at Grandpa's feet and began to massage them. He liked that. After a while he dozed off, but then suddenly Grandpa opened his eyes, and for a moment he just looked at his two beautiful granddaughters. Then, in a voice as tender and gentle as an angel, he said, "I'm looking at beauty, I'm feeling beauty; I think I've already gone to heaven."

Katie said it was as though her heart stopped at that moment. The Spirit was strong, as was the feeling of love. She had never felt closer to Grandpa.

When all the family was there that could come, Grandpa smiled at them and said, "I have to speak loudly because I have something important to say. Heavenly Father wants us to stay together. He wants us to return to Him. He wants us to love one another."

He leaned over to Grandma at this point, and he said, "Will you coach me?"

Grandma seemed to know what Grandpa was trying to say, because she then turned to the family and said, "He wants us to keep the commandments."

And then Grandpa began to sing, "Keep the Commandments." Grandma joined him, and one by one, each of their posterity joined in and added their voices. The power of the song increased, but so too did the power of love and the influence of the Lord's Spirit. It comforted, bound, and strengthened all who were present. It was as though the Lord was affirming to the family the truthfulness of this worthy patriarch's final message.

"I think I've said all I need to say," Grandpa concluded, "except that I love you."

To Katie, who watched all this, it was amazing how calm he was, how prepared he seemed to be. It's true—for the faithful, death holds no terror.

Grandpa smiled, picked up a white tissue, and said, "Is it okay if I wave goodbye?"

The family cried, hugged him goodbye, and Grandpa was gone shortly thereafter.

The impact this had on the family is immeasurable. Indeed, family and all that it righteously entails is forever.

I tell this story with permission, but you would have needed to have been there to fully understand. To this outsider, the impact this had on Katie is what most impresses me. She's never been the same since this incident.

"I knew," she said, "that Grandpa would be watching over me, and I didn't want to do anything to let him down." Then she repeated, "Grandpa's watching me. I don't want to do anything bad."

That is the power of family love. By the grace of God, may it grow in your home.

Love as Jesus Expressed It

Just this morning I ran outside to catch my six-year-old son as he walked to school. I felt something that I did not want to resist. I felt a warmth and an affection that I had to express. I caught up with him, pulled him into my arms tightly, and said, "I love you, Son." He responded, "I love you too, Dad." I then lifted him to the other side of an icy puddle too wide for him to cross, and he went on his way to school.

What is love? The dictionary defines *love* as a feeling or affection that we have for someone or something because of some benefit we receive. That kind of love is what the scriptures call "the love of men." It is the kind that waxes cold. We hear people say, "I love my family for all that they do for me." What happens when they stop doing, or we do not care for how they are doing it? Love dies, and the object of that love is replaced.

The love of God is different. It is pure, unfailing, and endures forever. I can only imagine how charged with emotion that upper room must have been on the night of the Last Supper. "A new commandment I give unto you," Jesus declared, "That ye love one another, as I have loved you, that ye also love one another. By this shall all men know that ye are my disciples, if ye have love one to another" (John 13:34–35).

But this is not a new commandment. It was given to Moses. What is new, then? From that day forward the Lord's disciples were to love with His love, as He loved. The old commandment was, "All things whatsoever ye would that men should do to you, do ye even so to them" (Matthew 7:12). But the new commandment is do unto others as Jesus would do.

Still, in the quiet of that upper room, Jesus continued, "If ye love me, keep my commandments" (John 14:15). Notice that He did not say, "If ye love me, tell me." The world is full of those who draw near with their lips, but their hearts are cold and distant. God's love is affection expressed with action. "This is my commandment, that ye love one another, as I have loved you" (John 15:12). "Greater love hath no man than this, that a man lay down his life for his friends" (John 15:13).

There it is. The highest expression of love known to God or man is to lay down one's life for another. The most perfect way to say I love you is to do for that person as God would. Perfect love is inspired love. Perfect love always involves sacrifice.

Within moments of teaching them this doctrine, Jesus put it into expression: "that the world may know that I love the Father, and as the Father gave me commandment, even so I do. Arise, let us go hence" (John 14:31). And hence was the Garden and the Cross.

They wanted him to stay. They grieved and wept over him (see JST, Mark 14:25). He was breaking their hearts, and He knew it (see John 16:6). But He knew that the greatest love He could express now was not what they wanted, but what God wanted for them. The Lord taught and cheered them as well as they could understand. He sealed them up unto the Father by His prayers and faith, and then left them for Gethsemane.

Gethsemane and Golgotha were the greatest expression of love this world has ever known. He poured out His soul unto death. He laid down His life for the Father and for us. He took that life up again and gave it to us forever.

Not all will receive of His love. Hardened hearts cannot feel it. Do not judge God's love by what you do not feel, for it is always there.

You may destroy your sensitivity to it by disobedience, but you can never kill His affection for you—not now, not ever.

Later, on the shores of the Sea of Galilee, the resurrected Lord asked Peter, "Simon, son of Jonas, lovest thou me?"

"Yea Lord;" Peter answered, "thou knowest that I love thee."

"Feed my sheep," came the Master's reply (John 21:16). His disciples mattered so much to Him that He gave His best for them. He still does!

You come to God and He fills you with His love and sends you out to give it away, starting with your family. You love them as you love them because you get to do for them, not because they do for you. This is love.

When Valentine's Day comes this year, before you say, "I love you," I hope you pray that what you do is what He would do.

Jedediah Morgan Grant

Years ago, I had the experience of standing on the high plains of Wyoming near the common grave of some pioneers. I did not know them or anything about them, yet there was a hallowed presence there I have not forgotten. I stand in awe of the stamina and heart of those who buried their loved ones and walked on.

"In the late summer of 1847, Jedediah M. Grant left Winter Quarters, Iowa, and set out for the Salt Lake Valley with his wife, Caroline, and his infant daughter, Margaret. Cholera broke out in the camp on the banks of the Sweetwater River in Wyoming. Caroline and Margaret became ill. Four-month-old Margaret died. Jedediah was forced to dig a shallow grave and leave his precious daughter behind.

"The death of her baby deeply affected Caroline, and her condition worsened. The camp fasted and prayed, but it soon became evident she was not going to live. Around midnight, she called her husband, Jedediah, looked into his face, and whispered, 'All is well! All is well! Please take me to the valley—Jeddy. Get Margaret—bring her—to me!'

"[Jedediah] answered tenderly and meaningfully as he sobbed with sorrow, 'Yes, yes, Caroline. I'll do my best. I'll do my best'" (Gene Sessions, *Mormon Thunder: A Documentary History of Jedediah Morgan Grant* [Urbana: University of Illinois Press, 1982], 68).

And she was gone—four days after her daughter. Jedediah built a coffin for his wife's body and drove day and night the remaining seventy-five miles to the Salt Lake Valley, where he buried her. The next day Jedediah, true to his promise and with his friend, Joseph Bates Noble, set out for Wyoming to bring back the body of little Margaret. After several days, they stood once more on the banks of the Sweetwater River.

Joseph Bates Noble recorded the following: "We stopped our rig where just a month previous a terrible night had been spent digging a grave in a driving thunderstorm. We now stepped forward, carrying the boxes and shovels. A few paces from the little grave we stopped hesitatingly, set down our things and stood with eyes fixed before us. Neither tried to speak. An ugly hole replaced the small mound: and so recently had the wolves departed that every sign was fresh before us. I dared not raise my eyes," he said, "to look at Jedediah. From the way I felt, I could but guess his feelings. Like statues in the wilderness we stood, grown to the spot, each fully realizing that nothing more could be done. After several moments of silent tears, we quietly withdrew carrying away again only that which we had brought" [Sessions, *Mormon Thunder*, 69).

Jedediah returned to Salt Lake knowing he had done his best. Many years later, shortly before his own death, Jedediah Grant was given the opportunity to enter the world of departed spirits. He saw many things. But significantly, the first person who came to him was his wife, Caroline, with their daughter, Margaret, in her arms. Caroline was beautiful.

"Here is little Margaret;" she said to him, "you know the wolves ate her up, but it did not hurt her; here she is all right" (Heber C. Kimball, *Journal of Discourses*, 4:135–138).

All around us today are those who fall, some physically from the effects of disease and death, others spiritually from the deadly effects of sin and addiction. We love them and nothing will ever change that, but are we going to languish in memory-laden misery? No!

Walk on! Bring honor to the memory of those you love, past and present, by getting up, in spite of the pain, squaring your shoulders, and going on, building the kingdom of God as you go. Carry on! Oh, carry on!

Source: Brent L. Top, "It Still Takes Faith," BYU Devotional, 22 July 1997, 9–10.

Martha And Mary

Have you ever noticed that there is a wonderful, dynamic tension in this world of ours? And *tension* is the right word. I mean, it's good for us to be busy and under pressure to measure up, but at the same time we're at high risk when we are feeling overwhelmed and under-qualified. Maybe you know the feeling. Happy and busy is wonderful; miserable and depressed is not. I guess it's like there's this path of perfect balance leading to exaltation, and the goal of life is not to be pulled off either side.

So how do we do this? How do we do all that's asked of us each day without losing the joy that makes it all worth doing? Maybe this story from the life of the Savior will help.

During the Savior's ministry, He and His disciples enter the small village of Bethany, just outside Jerusalem. The Master goes to the home of his close friends Martha and Mary. Immediately, Martha sets to work preparing to feed her distinguished guest, but Mary stays close to the Savior, sitting at His feet and listening to Him teach. After a time, the burden of the work becomes a little too much for Martha. Perhaps a little put out and impatient, she comes to the Savior and says to Him, "Lord, dost thou not care that my sister hath left me to serve alone? bid her therefore that she help me" (Luke 10:40). In other words. it sounds like she's saying, "Lord, don't you care that she's left me to do all the work? Tell her to get up and help me."

Tenderly, the Master replies, "Martha, Martha, thou art careful and troubled about many things: But one thing is needful: and Mary hath chosen that good part, which shall not be taken away from her" (Luke 10:41–42).

Notice that He never said that what Martha was doing was bad, only that what Mary was doing was more important at the time.

Most of us are like Martha. Our time and concerns are taken up with the busy work of life, and in a sense that's the way the Lord intended it. But remember: It is critical that we make the time every day to sit at the Master's feet, if you will, and be taught. Those moments of time we spend with God, praying and in the scriptures at the feet of the Savior, may be small by quantity, but their quality makes all the rest of life worth living.

Adapted from Luke 10.

Ahaz's Sign

More than seven hundred years before the birth of the Savior, the people of Jerusalem were frightened. Their peace was threatened by a ruthless power from the north, Assyria, who was taking over country after country. Judah's neighbors, Ephraim and Syria, were hastily forming political alliances to guard against the threat.

Judah's king, Ahaz, refused to join the alliance, choosing instead to bargain with Assyria directly for his nation's safety. The kings of Ephraim and Syria were angered that Ahaz and Judah would not join them and promised to invade and remove Ahaz as king. Isaiah the prophet came to Ahaz and told him not to fear the two allied kings, saying, in other words, "Don't listen to them; be at peace and trust the Lord." But the imminent political threat was too much for the wicked Ahaz. In his heart, he would not believe it. How could he? Their doom seemed sure in spite of Isaiah's promises.

Knowing that, Isaiah said, "Ask thee a sign of the Lord thy God; ask it either the depth, or in the height above." To seek signs of ourselves is evil, but when the Lord commands us to ask for one, it is evil not to. Moreover, to be told that His sign can come from the depths of hell or the heights of heaven, whatever He wants, must mean that God is very determined that this doubting man believe His promises.

Stubbornly, Ahaz refused to ask. Isaiah was disgusted with him and all his nation and said the Lord would give him a sign anyway. "Behold," he said, addressing himself now to all the nation, "a virgin shall conceive, and bear a son, and shall call His name Immanuel." The name means *God with us*.

A virgin bearing a son? That's impossible. Yet, God did the impossible on that first Christmas when Jesus was born. But Ahaz would not live to see the sign fulfilled.

Christ would not be born for another seven hundred years. So why was the sign given? Because this was not just a sign to Ahaz, but to all the children of God who doubt Him and His promises.

Every Christmas is a reminder that God did the impossible once, and He can do it again. Any who are troubled for any reason and seek peace need only look at the miracle of Christmas to awaken their latent faith. This is, ironically, the season of the coldest weather and yet for a time, it is the season of the warmest hearts.

When Christmas comes, "God is with us" again, in our hearts, our homes, and even our music. One need only look how our world changes this time of year to know that Christ is still in Christmas. Indeed, Christmas is an everlasting sign to a doubting world that God is still with us and that He loves us, and that He can still do the impossible, this time for you.

Sources:

- *See Sidney B. Sperry, The Voice of Israel's Prophets (Salt Lake City: Deseret Book, 1952), 28.*

- *Isaiah 7:2, 6, 9–14.*
- *Some have contended that virgin is not Isaiah's meaning, but rather an unmarried woman, but Nephi affirms that the impossible did happen: a virgin did conceive and bear a child. See 1 Nephi 11:18.*

Haircuts and Hugs

You remember that the Savior said, "Except ye . . . become as little children, ye shall not enter into the kingdom of heaven" (Matthew 18:3)?

That statement is true. So why are we trying so hard to get our children to grow up? From them we can learn much about what manner of men and women we ought to be. Let me illustrate.

I wanted a haircut. So, my wife and daughters gathered around on a Sunday night, and all gave their input as to how my hair should look. After the hair was cut, I let them teach me how to style it—what was left of it. It was a lot of fun and laughs!

When my haircut was finished, my little boy Adam hopped up on the chair and asked that his hair be cut exactly like Dad's. His mother complied, and soon his hair was just like mine. Then his sisters did to him just what they had done to me.

A little bit later, just before we went to bed, Adam overheard me mentioning that I was leaving for work around six in the morning. A few minutes later I heard him say that he was setting his alarm for six in the morning. When I asked him why he was getting up two hours early, he said, "So I can give you a hug before you go to work."

Little children are holy (see D&C 74:7). They're not capable of sin. The devil can't tempt them. They are whole and alive in Christ (see Moroni 8:12), and He adores them (see Matthew 18:16).

They are by nature what we must all become (see Moroni 8:10). They are trusting, full of love, and affectionate. They do not tend to arrogant, independent pride. They are quick to forgive and easy to be led (see Mosiah 3:19). In moments of discipline, if I could be as patient with Adam as he always is with me, we would do much better.

Perhaps all of us should worry less about making our children like us and try a little harder to be like them. There would be a lot less "maturity" that they would have to unlearn if we did. The more we are like our children, the more powerful with God we are (see 3 Nephi 11:37–39).

Now, the end of my story:

The next morning a sleepy, disheveled little boy met me as I was going out the door to work. He gave me a big hug and said, "I love you, Dad."

That's the son I want to be for my Heavenly Father. I want to get up early just to be with Him, and I want to be just like Him.

Jesus the Pioneer

July is a month of remembrance. It is a blessing to us that such a time is set aside where we may remember and honor the great patriots and pioneers of our past. It seems to me that the more we value what they did for us, the more sacred their memory becomes to us. In that spirit, if a pioneer is one who at great personal risk and sacrifice makes the journey first and opens the way for us to follow after, would you consider who may be the greatest pioneer in history?

Late on Friday afternoon after some six tortuous hours hanging on the cross of Calvary, the Lord Jesus Christ utters these final words: "Father, it is finished, thy will is done" (JST, Matthew 27:50); "into thy hands I commend my spirit" (Luke 23:46). And having said thus, the Savior of the world died.

Sometime before dawn on Sunday morning, the Lord returns in spirit to His body, and by the power of the Spirit of God, He raises that body from death and reenters it, never again to be divided. The angel of the Lord descends and rolls back the sealed stone from the garden tomb, but Jesus has already left.

As the signs of an impending sunrise become evident, Mary Magdalene and other women come to the tomb. They are greeted by angels, who announce, "He is not here: for he is risen" (Matthew 28:6).

A short time later, that same Mary is back at the tomb, this time alone and grieving. She supposes that someone has stolen the Lord's body. So inconceivable is the rising of someone from the dead, especially one whose body has been so thoroughly destroyed as was the Lord's, that the angel's words, "He is risen," just simply have not registered. The Lord approaches behind Mary. She sees Him but does not recognize Him. Supposing that He is the caretaker of that garden where the tomb is, she asks him if he has any knowledge of where the body of the Lord has been taken.

Then, the Lord says, "Mary" (John 20:16).

Something about the tone and tenderness by which He speaks her name causes her to recognize Him. She runs to embrace Him. The Lord stops her from touching Him and sends her to tell the disciples what she has seen.

Later that night, ten of the twelve are gathered, still skeptical of the many reports of the Lord's rising from the dead. As they are talking, the Master appears before them. So overwhelmed are they that they cannot believe their eyes for joy.

I don't believe it is accidental or incidental that in each case of the Lord's personal appearance after the Resurrection, there was a dramatic emotional shift from deep pain and doubt to indescribable joy.

If the pioneer whose efforts affect the most people for the greatest good for the longest time deserves the greatest adoration, then I submit that the Lord Jesus is the greatest pioneer of them all. Literally, all our hopes, our dreams, our loves and joy for all eternity, our happiness here and hereafter come because He went first and broke the bands of death. "[H]ow great the importance to make these things known unto the inhabitants of the earth, that they may know that there is no flesh that can dwell in the presence of God, save it be through the merits, and mercy, and grace of the Holy Messiah, who layeth down his life according to the flesh, and taketh it again by the power of the Spirit, that he may bring to pass the resurrection of the dead" (2 Nephi 2:8).

We may not understand it now, but someday I believe we will count His pioneering Atonement and Resurrection as one of the greatest gifts a generous God could ever have given.

Choose Ye This Day

Standing in their promised land, Joshua said to Israel, "choose you this day whom ye will serve; but as for me and my house, we will serve the Lord" (Joshua 24:15).

Every morning when we get out of bed, we stand at a crossroads. In one direction lies a destination of misery and self-recrimination; in the other lies a destination of happiness and personal power. The road between is paved with the commandments of God.

Recently, I was invited to participate in a conference of several hundred youth.

During one of my presentations, I held up a large stop sign that I had borrowed from the local city streets department. As I displayed it before them, I pointed out that it represented God's prophets and their teachings. I used the sign to illustrate that it is vital to our survival that we give careful heed to the prophets of God.

When I concluded my remarks that morning, a group of young people came forward to talk to me. One young woman approached me; I don't know who she is or where she was from, but I won't soon forget her. She was overcome with powerful emotion brought on by the Spirit. She threw her arms around me and clung to me, crying so hard she couldn't even talk. It was a tender moment of great joy for both of us.

The group dispersed, and I packed my stuff to go home. It took several trips to get it all loaded. On my second trip, I put the borrowed stop sign in the back of my pickup. While I was gone for another load and a quick errand, some young people from the conference saw the sign and stole it. It just so happened that witnesses saw it and immediately reported it to the police. When I got back to my truck, I was greeted by a note asking me to come to the police station.

To make a long story short, later that afternoon after the stop sign had been recovered and the thieves apprehended, I was in the police station when the officer walked in with a group of girls. I had no idea whether these girls were witnesses or suspects; I just knew they were connected somehow. I noticed, however, that one of those girls was sobbing very hard. I didn't know who she was or why she was crying, but I hurt for her. I stepped over to her; I put my arm around her shoulder and gave her a hug. She shed many tears that afternoon. I was later informed that that young woman was the one who had stolen my object lesson on the commandments.

That was an interesting day for me. I witnessed two sobbing young women: One who cried tears of joy because of right choices; the other, tears of deep pain and regret because of a foolish choice. Wickedness never was happiness, and never will be.

Righteousness always is.

Someday, I want a hug from the Savior. And when I do, I want His embrace and my tears to be borne of joy and the sense of victory, not pity, regret, and loss.

Again, "Choose ye this day, whom ye will serve" (Alma 30:8).

Little Dog

You've heard the phrase, "Choose you this day, whom ye will serve" (Joshua 24:15). Well, there is more to your personal choice than you may think.

My dad held the philosophy that every little boy should have a dog. So, when I was just a tot, he got me a mutt—a little Collie dog that we named Stockings. I still remember the long hours we played together, him chasing me around the yard, nipping my heels and tripping me up. We also worked together in the cows for years. He was a dog that well understood "sic 'em." He had no fear.

Since I was a boy who loved to wander, you can imagine the mountains and valleys a little man and his dog explored.

We went through much together. I grew up and he grew old. I was there on the day when a pack of dogs from a neighboring ranch attacked him, mangling his leg and tearing him up. I pulled him out of the fray and then cried and cried as he hovered for days between life and death. He recovered but was a three-legged cripple for the rest of his life. He was there for me when I was so sick for so many years with a bad stomach. We were the best of friends and did everything together. I loved him.

As I look back on it, Stockings had just one vice. He loved to chase cars. We tried everything to get him to stop, but he would not. It was his passion, and he was good at it.

He chased cars all his life, even on three legs, until one day the sheriff came to our house. In the back of his Ford Bronco was the broken body of my little dog. He had been hit by a car. He was still alive, but barely. We made him a soft bed on the sunny side of the house. For days I sat by him as he lingered and sank. Finally, my dad suggested that my mother take us to visit relatives. She loaded us up and we left town.

When we returned, I went straight for Stockings' bed, but it was empty. He had died just a couple of hours after we left.

Dad buried my best boyhood friend with fitting respect. I grieved and cried.

How I have wished that Stockings had chosen differently. His foolish choosing broke my heart and destroyed his life. So deeply did this affect me that never again would I set my heart on a pet.

It is with people as it was with a little dog—agency is not and never will be free. No man has a right to live wrong. Our choices always bring consequences to us and others. Someone here or in eternity is affected by our every choice. We are with each decision either drawing closer to God or further from Him.

To be an agent is to act and bind ourselves inexorably to an outcome. Therefore, wisdom is to get smart and then act that way. Oh, be wise in what you choose this day. Choose prayerfully, for even God stands aside for agency.

The Will of the Father

Every Father who seriously works to raise good sons will appreciate this story.

When the Savior appeared on the American continent after His resurrection, He announced, "I am Jesus Christ . . . and I have drunk out of that bitter cup which the Father hath given me, and have glorified the Father in taking upon me the sins of the world, in the which I have suffered the will of the Father in all things from the beginning" (3 Nephi 11:10–11). Notice that Jesus "suffered the will of the Father." No father ever had a better son than was Jesus.

At the tender age of twelve, Jesus reminded His mother, "How is it that ye sought me? Wist ye not that I must be about my Father's business?" (Luke 2:49). Twelve seems quite young to be so concerned about the saving of souls that He forsakes the security of family and friends. Yet, He loved His Father more than His friends.

At the beginning of His ministry, the Savior's Apostles returned with food for Him. Out of the distance came the people of a Samaritan city seeking His Living Water. To His caring Apostles, Jesus said, "My meat is to do the will of Him that sent me, and to finish His work" (John 4:34). In other words, "I live to do what my Father wants."

There is among men the devotion of the weak to a demagogue, but there never lived a mortal more powerful than Jesus. With His intellect and strength, Jesus could have usurped any Caesar and ruled the world, yet this mightiest mortal gave His heart and soul to obeying His Father in all things. It was the greatest example of faith and worship.

Indeed, at the very height of His glory and popularity among the Jews, Jesus announced, "I came down from heaven, not to do mine own will, but the will of him that sent me" (John 6:38). Then, by the Father's command, He taught doctrine that drove the fainthearted of friends away. It broke his heart, but He came not to be popular with men but with God. Through His personal sacrifice, Jesus proved His love for His Father, and thereby, His Father loved Him.

As He went to Gethsemane, Jesus declared, "That the world may know that I love the Father; and as the Father gave me commandment, even so I do. Arise let us go hence" (John 14:31). And He went to Gethsemane, the scourging and trial by the Jews, the cross of Golgotha, and, finally, the garden of the empty tomb. There are no words known to man, no language among mortals that can describe how much it hurt and how hard it actually was for Him to accomplish the will of the Father. How did He ever get through it?

When we ponder His Atonement and how hard it was, we may reach back into our memory for the greatest pain we have ever endured. Even if we reached beyond memory into imagination, still we could not comprehend His suffering and sacrifice. It was so much worse than even we can imagine—and all this because He loved His Father.

Jesus cried out, "Abba, Father, all things are possible unto thee; take away this cup from me: nevertheless not what I will, but what thou wilt" (Mark 14:36). He was not saying, "I don't like it and I don't want to, but if you insist, I will do it." No, He made the Father's will His will. His was a total surrender of will, of ego, and every vestige of pride and selfishness. A son who obeys his father is a good son. If He obeys grudgingly, that is acceptable, and if he obeys willingly, it is commendable. But a son who obeys totally and willingly is the best kind of son. Such a Son was the Lord Jesus.

Have we ever considered just how absolutely phenomenal it is that Jesus lived only to know the Father's will and do it (see D&C 19:24)? No matter the personal fatigue, hunger, inconvenience, pain, or personal loss, Jesus gave Himself to the Father and thereby, to us. Truly, He was incomprehensible not only in what He did, but in what He was.

In this light, consider what the Lord meant when He asked of us, "The Lord requireth the heart and a willing mind" (D&C 64:34).

"A New Heart"

In 2016, Brady was diagnosed with congestive heart failure. He would later learn that this and multiple heart problems were caused by a gene mutation. His heart was functioning at a mere 20 percent of capacity.

Initially, the treatment plan looked promising. With medications and other interventions, doctors felt that his heart could be strengthened, and he could live a long life with just a few side effects. The good news was that it worked for two years. His heart even got up to about 40 percent of capacity. Then one night, everything crashed. A late-night trip to the emergency room revealed that Brady was in end-stage heart failure. His heart was at less than 10 percent. For three days, Brady slipped in and out of consciousness. When he was finally stable enough, he was life-flighted to Salt Lake City for emergency surgery. On September 11, 2018, a partial artificial heart was installed to run the left side of his heart.

The surgery was very difficult. Brady was kept in a coma for several days to save his life, but the surgery proved successful and gave Brady needed time. He was added to the list for a heart transplant.

For the next seven months, Brady was in and out of the hospital multiple times a week. He waited. Then on Easter Sunday, 2019, he received a most miraculous phone call. They had found a heart. Brady records,

> What an amazing, meaningful time for me as I pondered what it meant to be born again. I reflected on my Savior's resurrection. I pondered scripture about having a change of heart, as I was about to have my stony heart removed, and have a new heart put in me.

It was during this time that Brady experienced a recurring dream. He found himself inside a large football stadium packed with tens of thousands of people, only a few of whom he recognized. Everyone was cheering for him. Everyone was holding up a sign that read, "We are praying for you, Brady," or other similar messages of encouragement.

At this stunning sight, Brady reflected,

> It was then that I realized I had been so sick and under medical comas etc. [that] . . . several times I physically could not pray for myself. I literally had thousands of people praying for me, including family members, friends, acquaintances, and people I didn't even know. I thought of all the prayer rolls in the temple alone as well as how hard my family worked to ask for prayers on social media.

The transplant surgery lasted thirteen hours and went well. Brady said when they finally woke him up that he had a hard time sleeping. His new heart was so loud that it felt like it was going to beat right out of his chest. He had never felt or heard his heart beat like that.

Today, Brady is healthier than he has ever been. He draws this powerful conclusion:

> We have the power to call down the blessings of heaven and pray for others and do something for them that they are incapable of doing for themselves. This principle applies to more than just people in a coma. There are many among us who, for several different reasons that we may not understand, lack the spiritual or mental or physical capacity to pray because of trials and hardships in their lives.

Indeed, "The effectual fervent prayer of a righteous man availeth much" (James 5:16).

The experience of Brady Ulrich, shared with permission.

The Divine Smile

Not long ago, I became curious and studied a large collection of artists' paintings of the Savior. I noticed that in nearly every painting, He was portrayed with a sober and serious expression. *Is this really what He's like?* I got to wondering. Is the Savior a cheerful and happy person, someone I would love to be around? Or is He stern and austere, someone who would scare me or make me tense to be around? Well, call me simple-minded if you will, but it was important for me to figure this out. I've settled the issue, at least in my mind. Let me tell you how.

First: Frequently in the scriptures, the Savior commanded His Apostles to "be of good cheer" (Matthew 9:2; John 16:33; Acts 23:11). I say "commanded them." And He told them that, even in the most trying of circumstances. He would not command them to be something that He Himself was not. He can't do that.

Second: I know that He's a happy and cheerful person by nature, because whenever I feel His spirit, I'm happy and cheerful; I love life.

Third: I searched through the scriptures and found only three references to the Lord smiling at someone—only three, but that was proof enough for me. But then I noticed something that deeply affected me. In all three of those references where I found the Savior smiling at someone, that person was in the act of obeying His commandments. Furthermore, in two of the three references, the people upon whom the divine smile shone were praying.

The Duty of Prayer

Some time ago, a bold student asked me a question that went something like this: "Why should I pray when it seems like no one's listening?"

That's a simple question. How would you answer it? For all who struggle with maintaining the habit of consistent daily prayer, I have a story.

Years ago, there was a young college student who struggled with his testimony. Through the powerful influence of others, his heart was touched, and he was convinced of the truthfulness of the gospel—*convinced*, not *converted*. He did not yet know for himself by the witness of the Spirit that it was true. But acting on faith, he went forward and was baptized. For many days after that, he prayed, he studied, and he yearned, but still received no witness as the Savior promised in John.

Late one afternoon while busily engaged in his studies, he became discouraged that he had not yet received an answer to his many prayers. The mood he was in became so oppressive that he couldn't study—couldn't concentrate. So, he went outside and wandered through the forests and fields near his home. The gloom of his mood, however, only darkened.

Finally, he realized that it was time for prayer. He had started a habit of going outside at a certain time and place each day for private prayer. But on this day and with this mood, he just did not feel like going to his grove to pray. "The heavens," he said, "seemed like brass over my head." One voice inside whispered that he should pray; the other voice enticed him away from his prayers.

Finally, after some struggle—or wrestle, if you will—he decided that he would keep his appointment with Heavenly Father. He knelt down, but no sooner had he opened his mouth than he heard something that resembled the rustling of silken robes over his head.

And then, all of a sudden, the Spirit of God descended upon him from head to foot, filling him with an indescribable witness and joy. All darkness and doubt were gone in an instant, and he knew that Jesus Christ is the Son of God and that the gospel is true. "I knew," he later said, "that God had conferred on me that which is of greater value than all the wealth and honors worlds can bestow."

From that day to the day of his death he was true, and he gave his life to the witness he had gained. And what a life it was—the obedience, the sacrifices, the miracles.

Lorenzo Snow was that young college student. He became a mighty man of God, all because of a day when he prayed because he was *supposed* to, not because he wanted to.

Remember: today, tonight, tomorrow, the rest of your life, "Go and do [thou] likewise" (Luke 10:37).

TYPING

I have a story for all those beloved and wonderful young people who are enjoying that rite of passage that we call "high school graduation." It's something of a parable, so pay close attention.

Many years ago, when I was a brash, young high school student, I remember that I was given the choice between two classes: One was typing (I think they now call it keyboarding), and I don't remember what the other one was. At the time, I think my reasoning went something like this: "Typing—that's girls' stuff! What in the world do I need that for? Not me, man, I'm not taking typing. Give me wood shop or something." I never learned to type, at all—never had a single lesson. At the time I never thought I'd need it.

I know that the Lord has a sense of humor, and I'm sure He's chuckled more than once watching me fumble through research papers and compositions in the wee hours of the morning with my pathetic, hunt-and-peck system of typing. I really tried to master that keyboard doing it "my way." Heaven knows that with a dozen years of college now, I've had enough practice, but it just wouldn't work! Oh, sure, I could go fast. I could sound like a hailstorm on a patio roof, but when it was finished, I dare you to read it. It would have taken a Urim and Thummim to translate it.

I'm here to tell you, "if you want to be a good typer, you gotta do it the way they tell ya." It may sound silly, but that one foolish, inconsequential decision has cost me more time and more frustration than you can imagine.

Well, I finally got fed up with it. So, thirty years after I should have made the correct decision, I decided to learn the correct way to type. My thirteen-year-old daughter sat down with me and said something like this: "Okay, Dad, these fingers go here, and these go here. These fingers cover these keys, and these fingers cover those keys. Got it, Dad? Good."

Simple, right? Not on your life! Do you think I could get those fingers to go where they were supposed to? Not a chance! It was like herding ten preschool children through a fun-house maze. And my little fingers were the worst. It was like they were a part of my body, but not connected to the same nervous system. I mean, think about it: How in the world are you supposed to concentrate on ten different things all at the same time? Trying to retrain these scarred, old hands has been one of the most frustrating physical things I have ever done. Trying to unlearn the effects of a bad decision is many times more difficult than to learn it right the first time.

Let me add this: Since that lesson from my daughter, I have experienced that wonderful phenomenon of a "proper conditioned response." I still need a lot of work, but now I can look at a word, and automatically—at least most of the time—the right finger will land on the right key at the right time, and I don't have to think about it. Ooh, that feels good!

You're graduating. Your decisions in the next few years will in large measure determine the course of your entire life. Make them wisely, make them very carefully, but most importantly, make them the Lord's way. If you form the right habits now, the manuscript you write of your life will be an epic adventure that you, the Lord, and your children will enjoy for centuries to come.

I close with these words from Ralph Waldo Emerson:

So nigh is grandeur to our dust,
So near is God to man,
When duty whispers low, Thou must,
The youth replies, I can!

A Child's Gift

Ancient prophets saw our day, and they saw our weaknesses. Among those things they foresaw is that we moderns would struggle with an inordinate love of money and "toys." Well, perhaps it is timely to remind us all of a principle that Jesus taught: "Lay not up for yourselves treasures upon earth, where moth and rust doth corrupt, and where thieves break through and steal: But lay up for yourselves treasures in heaven" (Matthew 6:19–20).

Now, what does that mean? What is a *treasure in heaven*? I hope this story will illustrate.

I know a young man we will call John. He wouldn't want you to know his real name. After finishing two years of faithful service to the Lord, he went off to college, where he worked days and went to school at night until he had completed a master's degree. Along the way, he married a sweet, supporting wife and started a family.

After graduation, John was handpicked out of a large field and was hired by a company developing new computer technology. The company was an instant success, and John came into a more-than-considerable sum of money.

But, back in Idaho, John's parents were struggling. They had mortgaged their own home to purchase another one for a daughter, and the deal had gone awry. Now these wonderful parents were reduced to working menial extra jobs just to keep from losing their own home.

One day John called home to talk with his mother concerning gift ideas for Mother's Day and Father's Day. During the course of the conversation, Mom shared her worries about this grinding debt that had disrupted their lives. At that time, it was the furthest thing from her mind to ask her son for help or to expect it from him.

Evidently, the news deeply troubled John, and he kept calling back to ask how much they needed to clear the debt. They were somewhat evasive in their answers, as you can understand. Finally, John put it straight to his mother: "Mom, how much do you need?"

Somewhat offhandedly, Mom said, "Well, about $77,000 would pay off this vacant second home."

She never expected what happened next. A few days later, a letter came in the mail. When she opened it up, inside was a check for $80,000 with a simple little note that said, "Pay off the house."

Well, Mom and Dad tried to give the money back. John wouldn't take it. They insisted that they would repay the money. But he wouldn't have that either. Finally, John told his somewhat overwhelmed and tearful mother, "No, Mom. I don't want the money back. Mom, go spend the money."

Well, Mom and Dad told me that they were so overwhelmed by so generous and loving a gift that they would be driving down the road, turn and look at each other, and just begin to cry when they realized that the debt was gone and their son had given them back their freedom.

They story doesn't end there—you see, there's a touching postscript to this story. John's aged grandparents live in an older, run-down, doublewide trailer in a small Idaho town. Their income is meager and fixed, and their health is declining.

One day Grandpa went to get the mail, when suddenly he called out to his wife, "Mother, come see this!"

Grandma came, and Grandpa handed her a letter from John containing a check for $20,000. Why? No reason, just to make their retirement a little easier. Grandpa and Grandma sat down right there and cried.

Now, my friends, "where your treasure is, there will your heart be also" (Matthew 6:21). "No man can serve two masters" (Matthew 6:24).

I ask you this: If the Lord or His servants came today and asked for all of it, could you give it?

The Lord bless you.

The Fatherhood of God

You know, it seems to me that, speaking of Father's Day, too often we focus so much on the Godhood of God that we fail to recognize the Fatherhood of God. Indeed, He is all-knowing and all-powerful and all-just. He governs the universe and holds the destinies of men and nations in His hands. But so, too, in every worthy sense of the word, He is a Father. He wants us to call Him Father. He is kind, gentle, loving, and solicitous of the welfare of us, His children.

Typically, when we think of the story of the prophet Jonah, we automatically think of a whale and how Jonah was swallowed for trying to run away from the mission that God had given him. And that's true; he was. But there's another element to that story that's worth telling.

You see, Jonah was a prophet during the time that Israel was ruled by Assyria, a ruthless world power. When Jonah is commanded to go to the city of Nineveh and call them to repentance, he attempts to run away—not so much because he just doesn't want to go (he's not lazy) but because Nineveh is the capitol city of Assyria, Israel's and Jonah's avowed enemy. What's more, Nineveh is a city of heathen Gentiles, another fact that makes them detestable to Jonah.

After the Lord manages to "adjust" Jonah's attitude in the whale's belly, Jonah goes to Nineveh and boldly and powerfully calls the city to repentance, saying, "Yet forty days, and Nineveh shall be overthrown" (Jonah 3:4).

Immediately—and our nation would do well to do similarly—the people of Nineveh begin to fast, pray, and bring themselves down in the depths of repentance. They are spared the destruction; God has mercy on them. But that mercy angers Jonah to the point that he goes to the Lord and asks the Lord to kill him. The Lord refuses, of course. So Jonah, pouting, goes outside the city and sits down on a hill and waits to see what will happen to the city.

The Lord decides to teach Jonah another lesson. The Lord causes a broad-leafed plant to grow up overnight over Jonah's head to shield him from the hot sun. Ah, the next day, Jonah enjoys that plant for its shade. But then a worm kills the plant. By the end of the next day, Jonah is suffering from heat stroke, and again he's angry with the Lord, this time for killing the plant. And again, Jonah's so mad he asks the Lord to kill him. At this point, Jonah is ready to be taught. The Lord comes to him and says, in essence, "Jonah, are you angry with me because I killed your shade plant?"

"Yes!" Jonah answers.

"Jonah, you feel sorry for that plant, yet you did no work to plant it or to nurture it. It grew up in one day, and it died in one day. You are angry with me because you wanted it to live. Jonah, shouldn't I have pity on a great city of 120,000 of my children who are lost and confused? Shouldn't I do everything I can to help them? Shouldn't I want them to live?"

The book of Jonah ends right there, but to me, this is a classic story. It demonstrates to me the Fatherhood of God. Whoever we are and wherever we are, He loves us, and He will do everything for us, His children, that we will allow Him to do for our happiness here and hereafter. I tell you, I love Him.

On Father's Day and on every day, could we do just a little more to remember the one we call "Our Heavenly Father," the One who has done so much for us?

Adapted from Jonah 3, 4.

Old Faithful

Over the years, I have observed some of the most arrogant, independent, and unlikely people fall to their knees and beg God for help in their times of trouble. I've often wondered why this is. I don't know all the reasons. But a recent experience in Yellowstone Park may shed some light on why they always go back there.

My family and I decided to be gawking tourists. We made it a point to see as much of Yellowstone as we could, and not from the car, either. One evening we toured Norris Geyser Basin. We learned that the world's largest geyser, Steamboat Geyser, is in that basin. It shoots water some three hundred to four hundred feet in the air. That's two to three times higher than Old Faithful. But its last major eruption was years ago, and it's anybody's guess when the next one will be. Well, from the sparse number of people and the lack of development in the area, it was obvious that Steamboat Geyser was not Yellowstone's star attraction.

The next day, we circled the lower loop of Yellowstone, stopping at various points of interest along the way, including Old Faithful. Now, it's been a lot of years since I was last at Old Faithful. I was astounded at the development that's occurred in that area. Not only were there palatial accommodations, but there were seemingly all the creature comforts and services available. It was a posh outpost in the pines!

Everywhere we went as we walked around the complex, we saw large clocks predicting Old Faithful's next eruption. With a heightening sense of anticipation, we made our way out to the huge boardwalk. Within a few minutes of the scheduled time, the boardwalk, benches, observation decks, and parking lots were crowded with hundreds and hundreds of people. We waited and watched our clocks, and suddenly, there it was, right on schedule—between one hundred and two hundred feet straight in the air against the backdrop of an azure blue sky. Oo-hs and aa-hs sounded up and down the boardwalk; cameras clicked. It was awesome! I don't think anybody went away disappointed. It was worth seeing.

I'd like to share part of a conversation I had with my daughter, Dawni Jo. She asked me a question that went something like this: "Daddy, if Steamboat Geyser is the largest in the world, then why isn't it as famous as Old Faithful?"

I thought about that for a moment, and then answered, "Because Old Faithful is faithful."

And so is God—He is faithful. He never changes and He never moves. He is constant; He is consistent. Sooner or later—and it's not an *if*, it's a *when*—we will all come to realize that He, God, has been and is all we really ever wanted from life in the first place.

Daniel

I don't think any of us would go get a job and then ask our employer on the first day for a year's wages in advance. That's ridiculous. You work for what you get, not the other way around. Yet there are some who expect great blessings and miracles from God without any effort on their part. Heaven knows how to put the proper price on its goods, and that price is faith and obedience. Daniel provides the perfect illustration.

By the decree of Darius, the Persian king, Daniel the Hebrew is unwittingly condemned to death and thrown into the lion's den. All night the king agonizes over Daniel, hoping that Daniel's God will spare him. Early the next morning, the king runs to the den and removes the stone.

"O Daniel," he said, "servant of the living God, is thy God"—and catch this line—"whom thou servest continually, able to deliver thee from the lions?" (Daniel 6:20).

And then as it were from the very jaws of hell itself, Daniel calls up, "O king, live for ever" (Daniel 6:21).

The king is so impressed by Daniel and his miraculous delivery that he sends forth a decree commanding all men everywhere to tremble and fear before the God of Daniel, "for He is the Living God," the king says. Daniel is subsequently restored to his high position in the government and enjoys great prosperity (see Daniel 6:26).

This is a story and a miracle so great that almost every child knows it. But how often do we teach why Daniel was worthy of such a miracle? What's the story behind it?

As a child, Daniel refused to violate the health code of his religion by eating the rich food commanded by King Nebuchadnezzar.

Because of that, not only did Daniel enjoy better health, but he was considered ten times wiser than any of the wisest men in Babylon. You know, he could have done what the rest of the crowd was doing by eating the food and drinking the wine, but he didn't.

Later, when the king decreed the death of all wise men in Babylon because they could not interpret his dream, it was Daniel who refused to roll over and accept death. He went boldly before the king, risking his life, and with the Lord's help interpreted the dream, thus saving many lives. He could have run away, but he didn't.

Again, it is the courageous Daniel who stands before two different kings, denounces them for their wickedness, commands them to repent, and prophesies their eventual fall from power. Now, either king could have killed Daniel in a moment by simply giving the word. Yet, Daniel feared God more than man, and boldly he told the truth.

Lastly, in his later life, Daniel had received and achieved all that the world could possibly offer: fame, fortune, power, and position, yet he sacrifices it all in a moment when he refuses to give up his daily prayers. This is a man of faith!

Throughout his life, Daniel was consistent; he was a consistent example of unflagging courage, faith, and integrity. Is it any wonder, then, that in his moment of need in the lion's den, his lifetime of faith was rewarded by the miraculous appearance of an angel who stopped the lions' mouths?

Faith precedes the miracle. May it be so with us that we don't come to expect something for nothing—either from life or from God.

Adapted from Daniel 1, 2, 6.

Elijah and the Widow

We live in the dark ages, in a manner of speaking. The world we live in is covered with gross spiritual darkness, and as time goes on, it's only going to get worse—more and more difficult to keep the faith. As one who has experienced those dark times, I can tell you they are terrible.

I ask you, how can we be sure we will not drift? How can we be sure that in that day when the Lord calls, we will be sufficiently attuned to answer His voice? Is there a key to spiritual safety? If ever there was a time to know what it is, it is now.

About 920 B.C., there lived a poor widow in a small Gentile village bordering Israel called Zarephath. Like everyone else, this poor widow suffered from the effects of a devastating famine brought on by the wickedness of God's covenant people. Her food supply dwindled until there was virtually nothing. Resigned to her fate, she went out one day to gather sticks to make a fire to cook the last of her flour into bread.

She was approached by a stranger who asked for a drink of water. Graciously she complied, and as she turned away to fetch the water, he called again to her, "Bring me, I pray thee, a morsel of bread in thine hand" (1 Kings 17:11).

She turned back and explained to him that she had only enough food left for one last meal for her and her son, and then they would die. How could you sit and watch your own son die? Can you sense something of the suffering and the despair that this woman endured?

The stranger then said, "Fear not; go and do as thou hast said: but make me [thereof] a little cake first, and bring it unto me, and after make for thee and [for] thy son. For thus saith the Lord God of Israel,

The barrel of meal shall not waste, neither shall the cruse of oil fail, until the day that the Lord sendeth rain upon the earth" (1 Kings 17:13–14).

What a request! How could anyone ask such a thing, especially of a starving widow and a tender child? If this man is an imposter, she will be trading her life and that of her son for a stranger.

I don't know what happened. Maybe this Gentile woman sensed something in this holy man. Whatever it was, she fed him first, and according to his promise, both her barrel of meal and cruse of oil never failed. They lived on miraculously for many days.

But as it is with us, her test wasn't over yet. She had yet more to prove—more to gain. Her son died suddenly, and in her agony of grief, she cried out to the man of God while holding her son and blamed herself. Tenderly the prophet reached and took the child out of her bosom and carried him up to a loft room, leaving the widow to her grief. She could not have known what was going to happen next. Death is, and always has been, permanent, but not now. Her faith and devotion to the prophet makes the impossible probable.

The man of God appears shortly thereafter carrying her son alive again and presents him to his mother. "See," he says, "thy son liveth" (1 Kings 17:23).

As she held her son, the mother cried out in faith and joy, "Now by this," she said, "I know that thou art a man of God, and that the word of the Lord in thy mouth is truth" (1 Kings 17:24).

That man of God was the great prophet of the sealing power, Elijah. And that woman was lifted up by the Savior Himself as an example to us all of faith (see Luke 4:25). What she did is what we must all do in trying times: Obey the prophets, and that with exactness. In mortality they may seem as other men, and in scripture they may seem larger than life. They are neither. They are men of God made powerful by Him. They are our only safety. If we hold to them, when it's all over, we too will live eternally with our sons and daughters and mothers and fathers—and our joy will be full forever.

Adapted from 1 Kings 17.

David and Goliath

The story of David and Goliath is a popular story in the Old Testament. David, whose name means "beloved" or "my beloved," enters the story as a rosy-cheeked teenager, the youngest of the eight sons of Jesse.

When Samuel came among Jesse's sons searching for Israel's new king, no one took David seriously enough to even send for him at first. And even after he was anointed, the incident seems to have been discounted by David's family: "David, a king?—ah!" Later, when Israel went to war with the Philistines, it was David who was left behind to tend the sheep.

One day Jesse sent David with food and supplies to the battlefront in the valley of Elah, some ten miles away, to find out how his sons were doing. David left the sheep in the hands of a keeper and made the journey.

He arrived among the men just as Goliath, the champion of the Philistines, walked out into the valley between the two contending armies. For forty days the two armies had been at a standoff, and every day, twice a day, Goliath came out and taunted and insulted the armies of Saul, calling for them to send out a man to fight. Rather than having the two armies fight, it was a custom of the time for the champion of each army to fight, and the victor of their fight was considered the victor of the cause.

But no one dared challenge Goliath, and who can blame him? According to our present text, Goliath stood over nine and a half feet tall. His armor weighed in at around a hundred and fifty pounds. The staff of his spear was like a weaver's beam, while the head of it weighed somewhere between twelve and twenty-six pounds. He was a part of the feared race of the Anakim and was a warrior trained from his childhood.

Well, David heard the blasphemy of the giant and was incensed, especially when the armies of Israel around him cowered in fear. "[W]ho is this uncircumcised Philistine," he said, "that he defy the armies of the living God?" (1 Samuel 17:26).

When David's brothers heard him, they were angry and scolded him for pride, naughtiness, and neglect of his duty at home. David's words reached the king, and David was brought before Saul. "Let no man's heart fail because of him;" David said, "thy servant will go and fight with this Philistine."

"Thou are not able to go against this Philistine," Saul said, "for thou art but a youth" (1 Samuel 17:33).

David pleaded for the chance to fight. Finally, the king said, "Go, and the Lord be with thee" (1 Samuel 17:37). When David entered the field, Goliath was insulted that they would send a mere boy. He cursed David by his gods and threatened to feed his flesh to the birds.

David's response to the giant allows us a glimpse into his great heart, wherein was the source of his power. He said, "Thou comest to me with a sword, and with a spear, and with a shield: but I come to thee in the name of the Lord of hosts. . . . This day will the Lord deliver thee into mine hand" (1 Samuel 17:45–46).

Enraged, the giant charged. David rushed to meet him, drawing from his shepherd's purse as he went a smooth stone, which he slung with a practiced aim. When he released that stone, it flew true and buried itself in the forehead of the giant, dropping him to the ground. David ran, pounced on him, drew out the massive sword, and with it slew the arrogant Philistine. The horrified Philistine army scattered with Israel in hot pursuit. It was not just a victory; it was a rout.

I love this story. It proves to me that if the cause is just, and there is faith in the God of Israel, what does it matter who scorns you or insults you?

Why do I tell this story? There are a lot of beloved, ruddy-cheeked youth. To them I say, "Welcome to the field, David. Goliath is waiting."

Adapted from 1 Samuel 16–17.

Stalled

Somewhere along the way in my educational experience, I was taught that objects in motion tend to stay in motion, and objects at rest tend to stay at rest. Well, a few days ago, I learned a powerful lesson about that.

I traveled to Wyoming in a large truck. It was a long trip. On my way back, I noticed that my fuel gauge was getting low. I did a quick calculation and realized I was not going to have enough fuel to get home. I decided to drive on and see just how far I could get. Before long, the gauge registered empty. I learned a long time ago not to trust old truck gauges, so I just ignored it and drove on. The problem with that was this was a 1998 Kenworth fresh from the factory. The gauge was fine!

I pushed on, after a while willing myself not to look at that gauge—trying to ignore it. Then, five miles from home, I thought I was going to make it. I stepped down on the accelerator, and instead of a responding surge of power, it choked and died. I rolled to a gradual stop on the side of the freeway.

There I was on a dark Saturday night at ten o'clock stalled on the side of the freeway, going up a hill, near a bridge, with a fifty-ton truck and a diesel engine out of fuel.

To make a long, pathetic story shorter, it took a lot of time, effort, anxiety, and the assistance of several people to get that engine started again and to get that monster off the freeway. My carelessness needlessly endangered myself and others. Fifteen minutes at a fuel stop would have kept me in motion and saved me more than two hours of grief, extra work, and stress.

Now, the point: Once we get on the path called "straight and narrow" leading back to our Father in Heaven, it is essential that we keep ourselves spiritually fueled so we can keep moving. Lingering unhappiness and discouragement are the indicators of low spiritual energy—a lack of fuel. They tell us that it's a critical time to fuel up.

How do we fuel up? Through searching the scriptures, fervent prayer, service to others, and any other activity that will bring the Holy Spirit into our lives. I am a witness to this truth: Speaking literally or figuratively, it is far easier to keep yourself in motion than to get started again once you have stalled.

"Are You a Mormon?"

In 1857 near San Bernadino, California, a young man, recently released from missionary service, was returning home to Utah. He had taken passage with a mail carrier and another man. They journeyed through the night, and in the morning they stopped for breakfast near a ranch. While the other two men began cooking breakfast, the young missionary went to tend to the horses.

Just then a wagon load of drunken men came into view. They were cursing and swearing, shouting and shooting, boasting they would kill the "Mormons." Their behavior was "almost indescribable and unendurable." They were a lawless mob such as only the West could see. One of them caught sight of the camp and made his way toward it.

The mail carrier and his companion hid in the brush, but the young man, unaware, strode into view. "The ruffian was swinging his weapon and uttering the most blood-curdling oaths and threats ever heard against the 'Mormons.' The young man said, 'I dared not run, though I trembled for fear which I dared not show. I therefore walked right up to the campfire and arrived there just a minute or two before the drunken desperado, who came directly toward me, and swinging his revolver in my face, with an oath cried out: 'Are you ___ _____ ____Mormon?'"

The nineteen-year-old lad "looked him straight in the eyes, and answered with emphasis: 'Yes siree; dyed in the wool; true blue, through and through.'"

The man's arms dropped to his side as if paralyzed—his pistol in one hand. The tone of his voice softened into "a subdued and maudlin" tone and he said, "Well, you are the ____ _____ pleasantest man I ever met! Shake," he said, and stuck out his hand.

"I am glad to see a fellow stand for his convictions." Then he turned and walked away to join his companions.

That young man was Joseph F. Smith, who later became the sixth president of the Church. Where did he learn such courage? From a father who faced a mob at Carthage and died for his testimony—Hyrum Smith—and from a mother who defied all odds, opposition, and adversity to keep her family together, bring them west, follow the prophets, and build her own mountain homestead of faith—Mary Fielding Smith. Courage is that quality that drives us to stand up, face our fears, and press forward.

Source: Gospel Doctrine: The Sermons and Writings of Joseph F. Smith *(Salt Lake City: Deseret Book, 1909), 531–532.*

Johann's Life

In August 1998, my friend Johann was diagnosed with advanced ovarian cancer. She was given three to five years to live. After radical surgery and nine rounds of chemotherapy, she was sure she had beaten it. But fifteen months later the cancer was back, even worse, requiring another surgery and six more rounds of chemo. Her hair fell out again, but this time the treatment didn't work. So her doctors sent her to Houston for additional help. But the doctors in Houston told her to go home and live out what little time she had left; there wasn't anything they could do.

With six children, nine grandchildren, and a son serving as a missionary, Johann felt that her work wasn't done. She wanted to live, but her faith and her will to fight were weakening. She began to wonder if God was hearing her prayers at all.

Then one morning she received a phone call. The caller was a man she'd never met before. His name was Neal A. Maxwell.

"I've heard," he said, "that you have cancer, and that you're having a few struggles—and I just wanted to talk with you. Is that okay?"

He went on to share some of his own experiences and several powerful verses of scripture.

"He was so kind. He never preached to me," she said. And as she spoke with him, she said, "It felt as though the Lord Himself was on the telephone with me."

When he asked if he and others could pray for her, she could scarcely answer, so deeply was she touched.

"We are going to pray," he said, "that your doctors will be blessed, and know the best treatment for you."

Well, the Spirit of the Lord came upon Johann, and her flagging faith in a loving Father in Heaven was renewed and returned. The doctors did find an experimental treatment, and today Johann is closer to the Lord than ever before—still alive and, more importantly, still living and determined to see her last missionary son come home.

Why do I share that story? Because in Matthew 5 Jesus said to His disciples, "Let your light so shine before men, that they may see your good works, and glorify your Father which is in Heaven" (Matthew 5:16). And then in the next chapter, He said, "when thou doest alms, let not thy left hand know what thy right hand doeth" (Matthew 6:3).

So, are our good works supposed to be seen or not? Well, in this darkened world of lost souls, Jesus is that light we hold up. His true disciples seek out the poor and the suffering, and they hold up Christ like a beacon before those people, and they beckon them to come to Him. But note: As they are holding Christ up, those disciples are looking up to Him also with reverence and awe. They are not looking admiringly down at themselves and their pose. They forget themselves.

Consider this: To do alms for the poor so carefully that our left hand doesn't notice what our right hand is doing not only requires that the world missed our part in the good deed, we missed it too.

And one more thing: In 1996, Elder Neal A. Maxwell began his own ongoing battle for life against cancer. When he talked to Johann, he knew first-hand the weakest that a person can be while still being alive.

Serve Thy Mother

There are only three known references to Jesus's direct interactions with His mother after His public ministry began. These references are very enlightening.

The Savior's ministry has just begun. He returns to Galilee from His baptism at Jordan and His temptation experience in the Judean wilderness. He comes with His disciples to a wedding feast at Cana. It may well have been a member of His family getting married, since it seems to be Mary who was in charge of the feast—we really don't know. But during the course of the festivities, they run out of wine. Mary comes to Jesus in her need and says to her son, "They have no wine" (John 2:3).

Does she know that He has the power to work miracles? Of course. Has He done it before? Of course. Jesus could have considered the request trivial and scoffed at it. But He doesn't. I love the way Jesus talks to His mother. "Woman," he says, "what wilt thou have me to do for thee? that will I do; for mine hour is not yet come" (JST, John 2:4).

Note: The use of the term *woman* in Jesus's day was not like we use it today. It was then a title of great respect. Even according to some, in this context, it was a reference to a woman of queenly caliber. It was as though He was saying to her, "Mother, I will do for you whatever you want. Your wish is my command." I like that.

And that is exactly what the Master does. Miraculously, He creates from water a more than ample supply of the highest quality wine to finish out the feast.

Now let me take you back. Remember what He said to her? "Woman, what wilt thou have me to do for thee? that will I do; for mine hour is not yet come." What did He mean by saying His "hour is not yet come"? Well, I wondered about this, so I studied it. Not surprisingly, it turned out that Jesus's hour was Gethsemane and Golgotha. He was born for that moment of moments when He would suffer and die to save the human family. So, in effect, the Savior was saying to His mother, "I can help you now, dear, but not then."

And yet—and this is so significant—when do we find the next major interaction between Jesus and His mother? It comes in the midst of His "hour." He is hanging on the cross of Calvary suffering an incomprehensible weight of agony, and from that cross He looks down where His aged mother stands with John, the beloved disciple. Both are grieving near the cross. He looks at His mother, and with the tenderest of concerns, He says to her, referring to John, "Woman, behold thy son!" (John 19:26). And then He looks over at John and says, "Behold thy mother!" (John 19:27). And from that hour, John "took her unto his own home" and cared for her (see John 19:27).

With the salvation of worlds innumerable, and of an infinite humanity weighing upon Him, I find it touching—overwhelming, in fact—that Jesus still had the time and the concern to see to the temporal salvation of His mother as one of His last acts of kindness before He died.

If only we would all do the same. Surely, it is no accident that Jesus's public ministry began and ended with tender acts of kindness for His mother.

Adapted from John 2, 18.

Run Away to Jesus

You know, there are times, I think, when we all feel like we're completely alone in a great big world, and that no one cares. A friend of mine recently shared an experience of a time when she felt like the whole world was against her. And as she told me that story of a time when she was just a little girl of about four years of age, she shared some profound wisdom that I'd like pass along. This is how the story goes:

Somehow Sarah got in trouble with her parents, probably for fighting with her younger sister. Obviously, she felt it had to have been Ashley's fault and not hers, but either way, she was disciplined and sent to her room. Oh, she was upset!—very upset at the injustice of it all!—and she decided she was going to run away.

She got her little Care Bear suitcase from under her bed, and she started packing to leave. The first thing she grabbed was her Barbie dolls. She stuffed them in. Then came her prettiest dresses. Once it was all in the suitcase, it was all Sarah could do to zip it up. But finally, all packed, she marched out and confronted her parents.

"I'm going to live with Jesus!" she announced. "At least He loves me!"

You can just see it, can't you? At this her parents smiled, and nodded, and said something like, "Okay, bye, Sarah. We'll miss you."

That was not quite the reaction Sarah wanted, and it infuriated her all the more. She stood there for a moment just hoping they'd give in. When they didn't, she turned and stormed out of the house in a snit.

Once outside, she started walking down the road. But then she realized she really didn't want to run away. I mean, after all, where's a four-year-old going to go? So, she went back to the house and sat down on the front steps. The problem now was, how was she going to get back in the house without her parents seeing her? She tried waiting until they went somewhere else, but they didn't budge. Finally, with no other choice, she tried to sneak back in. But her parents saw her, and, you know, they welcomed her back. Sarah tried this more than once until she realized this technique was just not working.

As she got older, Sarah thought of this as just a silly childhood memory. But then one day it struck her that even from the earliest age she knew that Heavenly Father and Jesus loved her, and that no matter how bad life became, she could always, in her words, "run away to Jesus."

How did she come to gain such important knowledge at such a tender age? I like the way Sarah said it. "How blessed I am," she said, "to be born with such incredible parents and teachers. I know that my Redeemer lives; I know that He loves me and will never leave me comfortless."

There are those who have temporarily forgotten what they once knew. They have forgotten, or perhaps never knew, how to "run away to Jesus."

Sarah is a grown woman now, and she says there are still times when she needs to run away. How does she do it? She opens the door to the scriptures and prayer—and by so doing, runs away into the welcoming arms of a loving and kind Heavenly Father.

Oh, my friends, it's true. You can do the same. Go on, run away.

The Adulterous Woman

I have a question: How does God really feel about us? I mean, after all, we're weak and fallen creatures prone to making mistakes. It seems to be a part of our fallen nature to be ungrateful and forgetful of all that He's done for us. So, with all of this, what are His feelings toward us, His unworthy children? There are many stories of the love of God, but there is one in particular that strikes a resonating chord with me.

It is early in the morning. The Savior has come to the temple to teach. A small group has gathered to listen to Him, when suddenly they are interrupted by a commotion. A group of men, scribes and Pharisees, approach the Savior, dragging a woman in obvious distress. They place her in the midst of this small group, and with a certain arrogance declare, "Master, this woman was taken in adultery, in the very act. Now Moses in the law commanded us, that such should be stoned: but, what sayest thou?" (John 8:4–5).

It was a trap, an ugly, ill-conceived trap. If He tells them to stone her, He will incur the wrath of the Romans who rule Jerusalem, and He will also be contradicting His own teachings about forgiveness, love, and a higher law. On the other hand, if He tells them to release her and let her go, He will appear to be contradicting Moses, the revered lawgiver of Israel, and He will incur the wrath of the people. The accusation they are leveling against the woman was insensitive and illegal. They had no right nor authority under Moses's law to do as they did. But in their mind, who cares? They have Him. There is no way for Him to get out of this one.

For a moment, step back and consider this woman. There is evidently no doubt of what she has done. But does she deserve this? I can imagine her broken in spirit, disheveled, and weeping at the public humiliation she is being forced to endure by evil men.

Well, to the surprise of the scribes, Jesus doesn't answer. He simply stoops down and begins writing on the ground as though He didn't hear them. In so doing, He draws all attention from the woman to Him. They gather around Him and press for an answer. Finally, at their dogged insistence, He raises Himself up and says, "He that is without sin among you, let him first cast a stone at her" (John 8:7).

His meaning is crystal clear: He that is without this same sin, adultery, among you, go ahead and stone her. Convicted by their own guilty consciences, they all slink off, leaving only the woman. Jesus raises Himself up again, and seeing none but the woman, He asks, "Woman,"—which, by the way, is a title of respect—"where are those thine accusers? hath no man condemned thee?"

"No man, Lord," she answered (John 8:10–11).

I love His answer: "Neither do I condemn thee: go, and sin no more" (John 8:11).

And the woman glorified God from that hour and believed on His name (see JST, John 8:11).

It is a principle of highest priority in our faith to *know* that God loves us perfectly, that our weaknesses and our mistakes when we are trying to obey do not anger Him. They draw forth His grace and mercy. I promise you, no matter what you have done, you are not beyond the boundaries of His love.

Remember what He said: "Come unto me, all ye that labour and are heavy laden, and I will give you rest" (Matthew 11:28).

Adapted from John 8:2–11.

Beloved Mother

All of us have what we have and are what we are because of the sacrifices of those who went before. Parents gave us life; teachers gave us knowledge; patriots gave us freedom. I wonder: Are we sufficiently appreciative?

My grandmother is ninety years old. I love her dearly. She has been my friend and teacher since I can remember. She's like a kindred spirit to me and has given me something very precious: a sense of my heritage, a tie to my past that I will forever cherish.

When she was just three years old, her mother passed away, and her father was unable to care for her, so she was raised by another family. I've heard her speak before in a voice filled with love and longing of a faint memory of a beautiful dark-haired woman walking through tall, meadow grass on a hill overlooking the Bear Lake carrying water for a flower garden. She remembers clinging to her mother's hand as they walked. And then, almost like a dream, that beautiful woman fades in the mists of a time-worn memory.

That is all I know of my great-grandmother.

Last summer while on vacation, my family came over the mountain into Garden City, Utah. Our plans were to play in the Bear Lake for a couple of days. As we were approaching town, a thought struck me with great force.

I said to my wife, "Hey, wait a minute! I think this is the town where Grandma was from when she was a child. My great-grandmother might be buried here!"

I felt an inexplicable sense of excitement. I could scarcely contain it. As soon as we were settled in, I began making phone calls to see if I could get directions to the cemetery. Finally, by late that afternoon, we found the cemetery situated in the hills above town overlooking the Bear Lake. It was a beautiful spot.

I divided the children up, assigned each of them a row of markers, and we went looking. I wasn't even sure we were in the right town, let alone in the right cemetery. It wasn't long before Sharise let out a triumphant yell, "I found it!"

We all came running, and sure enough there it was: *Ann Mayne, Beloved Mother, 1872–1910.*

Well, the novelty soon wore off for the children and they scattered to explore. But me? I didn't want to leave. I know this sounds kind of strange, but it was like I found a connection to my past, like a dim memory was becoming a living reality.

As I sat and wondered about my great-grandmother and what she was like, my attention was suddenly drawn to the western sky. The setting sun had burst through a hole in the clouds, sending brilliant streams of light in all directions and lining the clouds all around with a beautiful, luminescent silver. Oh, it was breathtaking!

As I stared in awe, the Spirit of God came over me, and I felt an assurance that someday this grave would be thrown open, and this beloved mother would come forth with resplendent glory, shining like the sun to rejoin her family, never more to be separated. To me it was a sign of things to come.

I have to say I still don't know much about my great-grandmother, but now I feel like I know her. I end where I began.

All of us in the present stand on the shoulders of those in the past. May we not forget them, as I am confident they have not forgotten us.

The Pharisee and the Publican

I want to tell you a true story that never actually happened. It's a parable told by the Savior about two men praying in the temple. And one of these men has become my hero, someone I'm trying, rather unsuccessfully, to be like.

One of the men is devoutly religious. He works with great diligence to be strictly obedient to all the commandments of God. He is greatly respected and admired by the people around him. So faithful is he that he pays a larger tithe than is asked and fasts twice a week—far more than is required.

The other man seems to have been somewhat dishonest in the past. He is despised and dishonored, even outright rejected by his fellows. By some he's considered to be a traitor to his country. And there even seems to be evidence that he has cared little for God and His commandments, up until now.

Which of these two is my hero? Well, you might be shocked, but it's the second man. Why? Well, I once heard that out of the abundance of the heart the mouth speaketh. Listen to these fellows as they pray.

The first man, a Pharisee, a religious leader among the Jews, prays as follows:

"God, I thank thee, that I am not as other men are, extortioners, unjust, adulterers, or even as this publican. I fast twice in the week, I give tithes of all that I possess" (Luke 18:11–12).

He sounds pretty sure of himself, doesn't he?

Now hear the prayer offered by the second man, a publican; he's a tax collector. He feels so unworthy that he beats on his chest; he won't lift his eyes or even stand near the devout Pharisee. He prays simply, "God be merciful to me a sinner" (Luke 18:13).

To this publican's prayer, the Lord responds, "I tell you, this man went down to his house justified rather than the other" (Luke 18:14).

This man, the publican, is my hero because no matter what his past has been, his present is humble and repentant—not arrogant, not self-righteous. Thus, he is right with God—and at any cost, that's what I want to be.

May God grant such a happy quest for all those who seek it.

Adapted from Luke 18:11–14.

The Tire Guy

I have lived long enough to see my own faults and failings manifest themselves in my adult children. And I want you to know that's a humbling experience, especially when you know that nothing you can say now is ever going to fix it.

I heard once that someone said more religion is caught than taught. I believe that. How does that work? Well, let me show you.

After an already long day at work in western Wyoming, I was on my way home in a large truck. Just a few miles north of Palisades Reservoir in Idaho, I suddenly felt the truck jerk.

What was that? I thought.

I scanned the gauges and looked down; I didn't see anything, and the truck was running normally again, so I just went on. About a half a mile later, I happened to glance in my mirror and saw billows of smoke rolling out from under the back axle of my trailer.

I pulled over, but it was too late! All four tires on the back axle of my trailer were as ruined, flat, and deflated as my ego. Evidently a piece of pressed board had been dropped on the highway; it had flipped up when I passed over it, hitting my brake line and tearing it off. Well, that caused a loss of air pressure, and with a loss of air pressure, the brakes locked up and turned the tires into smoke and mush.

With the help of a kind sheriff's deputy, we moved the impudent beast off the road, and a guy was dispatched from Les Schwab Tires in Idaho Falls to come and get me on my way. I sat in the cab of the truck to wait and take stock. It was getting dark. The temperature was dropping like a rock; it was *cold*. Dark, heavy clouds hung over all the mountains, and to make matters worse, I was tired, all alone—and I had the mood of a pickle sucker. You can imagine! And to make things worse, I just finished eating a cold supper.

And then the tire guy pulled up. I don't know what I expected, but out of the cab stepped a very ordinary-looking fellow. I could tell by his clothes that I wasn't the only one who had had a long day of work! Nonetheless, he greeted me cheerfully.

He took one look at the situation, and after he saw my blunder, I expected some comment about the "loose nut behind the wheel"—but the comment never came!

He went to work immediately, and while he worked, we chatted. I made some comment about coming all the way out here. He looked up at me with a grin and let me know that he had been on overtime for some time, but there was not the least impression that he was putout by having to come and rescue me.

I like you! I thought.

I began to notice after a while not a word of profanity or vulgarity came out of that man's mouth. In the whole time we were there, he said not a single negative thing about another person. He was cheerful; he was positive; he was quick to laugh. There was no arrogance; there was not the least bit of attitude of being better than anybody. He was as down-to-earth and genuine as any man that I have ever met.

He made some comment, just in the course of conversation, about driving to church on Sunday. And no, it was not dropped as a lead-in to a proselyting pitch. It was just a simple statement of fact. When he learned that I was a little bit on the religious side myself, he shared a sweet, faith-promoting experience that had happened to him and his wife. It was tender; it was appreciated; it was wonderful. *This is a good man,* I thought, *a very good man.*

You need to know he was not trying to impress me.

He saw nothing in me to impress—trust me! And he had no idea who I was; I never told him my name.

Once the trailer was repaired, we shook hands and I drove off. A few miles down the road, I took stock again. My mood and my attitude were completely different. I felt happy, cheerful; I felt warm inside.

It was Rex. The spirit of the Lord was with him. He had cheered my soul and built my faith—a true disciple of the Lord Jesus Christ in dirty clothes changing tires on the side of the road. Is there a lesson there? You bet there is!

I'm asked all the time where I get my stories. Well, this is where I get them—from the wonderful people I meet and watch. You must know that you cannot hide what you are behind the words you say or the clothes you wear. Every person you meet can feel your spirit for good or ill. If you would be a missionary, then you must be Christ-like. If you would lead your children to Christ, then you must give them a light to follow. And lastly, with some humor, be careful. You never know who is watching and the power they have.

Rex, thanks! You're a Saint, brother.

And to your employers, give this man a raise! He'll do more for your sales than all the free beef you can pitch!

THE BREAD OF LIFE

As the second Passover of the Lord's ministry drew near, word reached Him that John the Baptist, his friend and forerunner, had been murdered. Seeking solitude, Jesus and His disciples withdrew from the multitudes to the other side of the Sea of Galilee. However, the crowds saw Him go, and they ran around the lake ahead of Him and were waiting for Him when His boat touched land (see Matthew 14:13).

Filled with compassion, Jesus spent the day teaching and ministering to them. That evening, the disciples came and asked Jesus to send the people away into the villages so that they might obtain food. He answered and said unto them, "Give ye them to eat. And they say unto Him, Shall we go and buy two hundred pennyworth of bread, and give them to eat?" (Mark 6:37).

A penny was a day's wages for a working man (see Matthew 20:1–2). Evidently, the crowd that had gathered was huge.

Jesus commanded the disciples to have the men sit down on the abundant green grass in companies of fifties and hundreds. After He looked up and gave thanks, He began to break the five loaves and two fish and filled the baskets of the disciples, who then distributed the food to the hungry multitude. Everyone ate, and everyone was filled, and what's more, everyone saw the miracle. Twelve baskets of leftover food were gathered, more in quantity than the original five loaves and two fishes. The people were so moved by the miracle that they proclaimed Jesus as the Messiah and tried to forcefully make Him king (see John 6:15).

At this point, the Lord was at the height of His popularity and renown. He was known the length and breadth of Israel and beyond.

Thousands of people flocked to see Him and hear Him. But all that was about to change.

Driven by their stomachs, the crowd followed Jesus and found Him the next day in Capernaum in the synagogue (see JST, John 6:26). Their amazement at His presence across the lake is turned to anger at His audacity as He declared to them that He is "the bread of eternal life"—that without His flesh and blood, they would have no life in them. The people murmured; even some of His disciples murmured. "Is not this Jesus, the son of Joseph, whose father and mother we know?" (John 6:42).

The doctrinal diet is too much for them. They think they know Him too well to accept Him as so much. The scripture records that "From that time many of His disciples went back, and walked no more with Him" (John 6:66). From this pinnacle of popularity, Jesus descended all the way to the utter aloneness of the cross.

There are perhaps some who will say, "I will not do as others have done. I will never leave the Savior." Others have said that, and they have left. What can we do to ensure that we are not among those who desert Him—leave Him when the fire gets the hottest?

I have an answer for you: Jesus said, "I am that bread of life" (John 6:48). Notice that the Master did not say, "I am the coat of life." He said *bread*. Bread is the staff of life. It's the bulk of our diet. It is strength; it is energy; it is life. We do not put it on when we need it. We take it into us continually, and it becomes a part of us; it becomes us. So should His words, His commandments, His example be what we live on until He becomes us. If you would endure, take Him in, all of Him, and all the way—no half measures.

Based on Matthew 14 and John 6.

Only God Gives As

You know, sometimes life would be so unfair if we didn't have an omnipotent friend for a friend.

Bret entered the university majoring in English with his eyes set on going to law school, but he would have to get straight As in order to get in. Well, that's all well and good, but unfortunately one of his professors was on a personal crusade to combat grade inflation. Not only that, but Bret was the only religious person in a class full of agnostics.

Bret worked for two weeks on their first writing assignment, outlining, writing, and rewriting his paper. But when it came back, the grade was a C. Bret was sick. He approached the instructor and asked what it would take to get an A.

With a sneer, the professor replied, "Only God gives As." The professor then added that a paper would have to be suitable for publication in order to get an A in his class.

Now, that's encouraging. With the next assignment they were given one week to analyze a novel. It couldn't have come at a worse time in Bret's life. He had commitments for the rest of the week; every day was tied up; there was no free time. And he had too much integrity to renege on the commitments he had made. Even Saturday, he spent the day doing yard work for an incapacitated family. By Sunday, he was in trouble, and he knew it; he had done absolutely nothing on the paper. Surely, this was a classic example of the ox being in the mire. The Lord would understand if he wrote the paper on Sunday, wouldn't He? He was sorely tempted.

But then he remembered the promise he had made to the Lord that he would never do homework on the Sabbath. He set the paper aside and made plans for Monday morning. As he did so, he asked the Lord to strengthen and help him. Monday morning, he had a scant two hours, one of which he spent brainstorming and the other typing. There was no time for revisions or corrections, or even a hello as he gave it to the professor. He turned it in fully expecting to get it back with a failing grade, but at least there was the assurance that he had done his best. No matter what happened, he was square with the Lord.

The next week he came to class. The essays were on the corner of the teacher's desk. As usual, the professor waited until the end of class to pass them out, which was just fine with Bret; he was in no hurry to get it back. As the class closed, the professor picked up the stack of papers and just stood there flipping through the pages of the paper on top of the stack. Finally, he looked up. "Class," he said after a moment, "I suppose I have a reputation for being a hard grader. Well, I want you to know that today, for the first time in my teaching career, I have awarded a student an *A+*."

He handed out the papers. Bret looked down at his grade. It was an *A+*.

"I, the Lord, am bound when ye do what I say" (D&C 82:10).

Perhaps the professor was right after all, Bret thought; *only God gives A*s.

Stanford and Arabella

January 26, 1880, Joseph Stanford Smith and his wife, Arabella, stood with others at the top of the treacherous crevice known as "Hole-in-the-Rock" in Southern Utah. They had to get down. Using ropes, pulleys, logs for brakes, and with men holding the wagons back, they lowered each wagon carefully down the steep, treacherous slope. Stanford was at the bottom, helping ferry the wagons across the river.

Finally, word came that all the wagons were down. Stanford looked around. His wagon was nowhere to be found. It had been moved back and overlooked, and it had been left at the top.

For a moment, Stanford's face flushed with rage. He threw his hat on the ground and stomped on it, as was his habit when he was angry.

"With me down there helping get their wagons on the raft, I thought someone would bring my wagon down. Drat 'em!" he said.

"I've got the horses harnessed and all the things packed," Belle breathlessly assured him.

Stanford tied his mule, Old Nig, to the back axle of the wagon to slow it down. Then he cross-locked the wheels with chains.

They walked to the top of the crevice, where, hand in hand, they looked down at ten feet of loose sand, then a rocky pitch as steep as the roof of a house and barely as wide as the wagon. Below that a dizzy chute led down to the landing place.

It was that first drop of 150 feet that frightened him.

"I'm afraid we can't make it," he exclaimed.

"But we've got to make it," she answered calmly.

"If only we had a few men to hold the wagon back, we might make it, Belle."

"I'll do the holding back," said Belle, "on Old Nig's lines."

Arabella removed the children from the wagon and tucked them in a safe place with quilts wrapped around them.

"Don't move, dears," she said. "Don't even stand up. As soon as we get the wagon down, Papa will come back for you!"

Stanford braced his legs against the dashboard, and they started down through Hole-in-the-Rock. The first lurch nearly pulled Belle off her feet. She dug her heels in to hold her balance. Old Nig was thrown to his haunches. Arabella raced after him and the wagon holding to the lines with desperate strength. Nig rolled to his side and gave a shrill neigh of terror.

Belle lost her balance and went sprawling after Old Nig. She was blinded by the sand, which streamed after her. She gritted her teeth and hung on to the lines. A jagged rock tore her flesh and hot pain ran up her leg from heel to hip. The wagon struck a huge boulder. The impact jerked her to her feet and flung her against the side of the cliff.

Finally, at the bottom of the chute, the wagon stopped. Stanford jumped off and ran back. His first sight was of Old Nig, bloodied, bruised, and barely alive. Then he saw Belle—still holding onto the reins, blood streaming from her leg and covered with dirt from head to toe. They had made it. They were safe! They were safe!

"Darling, will you be all right?" Stanford asked.

"Of course I will," she said. "Just leave me here and go as fast as you can for the children."

"I'll hurry." He began the steep climb up the incline they had just come down. He slowed down and looked around. He had driven a wagon down that fearful crevice and dragged his wife behind; God bless her gallant heart! He kicked the rocks at his feet, and with tears streaming down his face, lifted his hat in salute to Arabella his wife.

As told by a grandson, Raymond Smith Jones, in David E. Miller, Hole-in-the-Rock: An Epic in the Colonization of the Great American West *(Salt Lake City: University of Utah Press, 1966), 111–114, as cited in Brent L. Top, "It Still Takes Faith," BYU Devotional Address, July 22, 1997, 10–11.*

The Swings

I have a simple story for all those young people who are graduating and moving on with their lives.

My children have always enjoyed going to the park and playing on the equipment, especially the swings. Not long ago, we stopped by a park while on a camping trip, and it wasn't long before they found the swings and began to say, "Push me, Daddy, push me!"

I went down the line pushing each child in turn until they were all going. After I got them going, the older children pretty well kept themselves swinging high. Once in a while they'd ask me to give them a push, but they could mostly handle it themselves. But the younger ones nearly wore me out! I'd get them swinging, and then they'd just sit there and swing back and forth, back and forth, until they slowly swung to a stop. Then they'd cry for me to get them going again. It wasn't long before Dad was ready to move on to the teeter-totter.

I well remember those days when they were all young and they all needed to be continually pushed. I have to say, I miss it just a bit, but I'm grateful now that my older ones have learned how to pump themselves and stay up high.

My dear young friends, since you were a baby, parents, teachers, and friends have been pushing you higher and higher—and along the way we have hoped beyond hope that you would learn how to pump yourself. We knew the day would come when you'd leave, and we would no longer be there to push you. Now it's here, and though you may be excited to go, and I suppose you should be, there are those who hurt and pray that you've learned. May the grace of God go with you.

"Arise and Read the Eleventh Chapter of Isaiah"

On August 6, 1832, in Benson, New York, Ira Ames was on his way to a general conference of the Church. He stopped along the way to spend the night with family. There were a number of neighbors visiting at his uncle's house that night. Their conversation over the course of the evening turned to cutting ridicule and outright slander of Joseph Smith and the Church. Their anti-Mormon comments had deep effect on Ira as a new member of the Church. He records,

> I was in deep anguish of mind. Their conversation and spirit had seemed to get control over me. I knew not what to think nor what to believe: I was in agony. When I retired to my bedroom, I bowed myself down in anguish before the Lord and besought him in [mighty prayer] and faith to give me a testimony of the truth of this work. I wrestled sometime and then went to bed and slept.

Somewhere in the early morning hours, Ira experienced a dream in which a personage appeared to him as he was sleeping and said, "Arise and read the eleventh chapter of Isaiah." The personage went away; soon after, he came again, repeating the same words. The angel came a third time and said, "Arise and read the eleventh chapter of Isaiah to confirm you of the truth of the work."

Ira woke immediately and saw a large Bible at the head of his bed. He opened it, having no idea what was in Isaiah 11, and began to read. He recorded the following in his history:

I read it and the Spirit made me understand the latter-day work pictured in that chapter. I was satisfied and felt to rejoice and thank the Lord for his kindness in manifesting this thing to me and I told him it was enough.

It was enough. Ira put his questions and doubts behind him and went on to a lifetime of dedicated service in the kingdom of God.

It's normal to have doubts and questions about the Church, Joseph Smith, and the Restoration in general; perhaps it's even expected. We are appointed to learn line upon line and precept upon precept, here a little and there a little. It is not all to be understood at once. Moreover, it is not the responsibility of the Church or its leaders to answer our every question of doctrine or history. That is between us and the Lord, and it is our salvation.

But what Ira did is instructive. He humbled himself in mighty prayer before the Lord and then turned to the scriptures. The angel did not settle his doubts or answer his questions; Isaiah did that. And so will the holy word of God do for each one of us. And, by the way, Isaiah 11 is one of the most powerful and profound chapters on the Restoration in all of holy writ. Portions of its teachings are so powerful that I have never dared share them in a classroom or public setting.

Source: Ira Ames Autobiography
https://www.familysearch.org/tree/person/memories/KWJP-FR4

Hall Family Prayer

As strange as it may sound, I believe that every person has an aura. This aura radiates from them to affect for good or ill everyone who comes in contact with them. Now, not only is this true of individuals, but so also is it true of families and homes, especially those obedient to the Lord in family prayer and scripture study. This I have learned by my own personal experience.

Years ago, as a young college student, I was invited one weekend by a beautiful young woman to go with her and her family on an outing. I scarcely knew her, and I didn't know her family at all.

We arrived late, introductions were made, and I was given the den in which to bed down for the night.

I remember the next morning that I awoke early, and I heard something of a commotion from outside my room coming from the direction of the family room. When I went out to investigate, I was promptly invited to participate with the family in family prayer and scripture study. Now, you have to understand that religion at this time for me was a relatively new thing. I was amazed! I had never actually seen such a thing take place before, especially like this.

As I looked around the room, I saw those two wonderful parents holding children on their laps, and eleven children ranging in age from about four up to twenty-one, all awake and in various stages of alertness, and all but one of them was fully dressed and ready for the day's activities. All of this was at a time of day on a Saturday morning when most people are still asleep.

Well, I don't know if anyone in that family remembers that day, or that I was even there, but I know I'll never forget. I felt the Spirit of God in that home that day, and I was deeply moved by the love and acceptance I felt from them. They helped change the course of my life. They had such an impact on me that day that I vowed then and there, God willing, that I would do all I could to create such a home of my own. Heaven only knows how I've done.

The Widow of Nain

To have compassion is to feel an emotion that combines love and pity. This story is about the compassion of Jesus Christ.

One day the Savior was approaching a beautiful mountain village called Nain. A large crowd accompanied Him, including many of His disciples. As they neared, they came upon a funeral procession. Many of the people filed in mourning with the grieving mother. The man being buried was her only son, and her tragedy was compounded by the fact that she was a widow.

Jesus saw her, and He perceived the situation immediately. As always, concerned with the plight of the widow, the Savior was filled with tender compassion for her and He said to her, "Weep not" (Luke 7:13).

He turned from her and "touched the bier . . . that bare . . . [her son's body]" (Luke 7:14). Those who carried the bier stopped when Jesus did this. Jesus then shocked them when He said, "Young man, I say unto thee, Arise" (Luke 7:14).

The dead man sat up and began to speak. Luke then records these meaningful words: "And [Jesus] delivered him to his mother" (Luke 7:15). Can you imagine? What a gift of joy He gave that woman!

A worshipful reverence came upon the people and they glorified God and proclaimed that "God hath visited his people."

Now step back from the story for just a moment. Why did Jesus do this? Did the Savior perform such miracles every time there was a need? No, He didn't. So why was the lost son returned to the widow? Well, simply because the Savior had compassion on her—He felt sorry for her, and giving her back her son was the greatest eternal good at that moment.

It was the Widow of Nain who was singled out and so blessed. We do not know all the reasons why this story ended so happily when others have not. Maybe we'll never know in this life. But know this: "[God] doeth not anything save it be for the benefit of the world." He always does the greatest good. He is always just.

Some of us don't get the miracles we want. Does He care about us any less? Absolutely, not! His love and His compassion for us are perfect and ever present. The time will come when you and I will all see the salvation of the Lord, and "confess before [Him] that His [ways] judgments are just." But for now, let us be patient until we are perfected in Christ Jesus, and may we be allowed to see as the Father does.

The Comforter

On His last night in mortality, Jesus promised His disciples another comforter. He had been their comforter during His ministry, but now He was going away—but not before He assured them that He would not leave them as orphans.

It is no accident of translation that Jesus called the Holy Ghost *the Comforter*. What is this Comforter, and how may I receive Him? This powerful and simple story will illustrate; it comes from the life of one of my friends and former students.

Meggan was eleven years old. Among Meggan and her friends, one of the coolest things you could do was babysit. I can't for the life of me figure that out, but I suppose it must have been a mark of a mature young woman if she could be trusted to be a babysitter.

One night, Meggan was asked to babysit her nephew. Oh boy!—wait till the next day, when she could tell her friends. Everything was going great. At first, they watched movies, they played with toys, they had a great time, and everything was under control.

But then—and only a parent would fully understand this—it came time for bed. Meggan took little Zack upstairs and began to rock him to sleep in the rocking chair. But instead of settling down, Zack began to cry—hysterically. And nothing Meggan tried to do settled him down. Finally, out of frustration and panic, she almost began to cry herself.

Then she remembered her parents. She left Zack upstairs, and down the stairs she ran and called her parents. The phone rang and rang. No one was home. By now, Meggan's fear had given way to terror. She ran back upstairs to check on Zack, and he was still screaming. She stood there wondering what to do; her tears overflowed, and she began to cry.

Just then, she heard a knock at the door. Frantically, she raced down the stairs, thinking it was her parents. But when she opened the door, there was no one there. Oh, that was it! That pushed her over the edge. Meggan dropped to her knees and asked Heavenly Father to help her calm Zack and to comfort her as well. She finished that heartfelt prayer and she stood up.

At that moment, she heard a gentle, comforting voice from upstairs calling her name, "Meggan, Meggan."

Following the voice, Meggan went back upstairs to Zack's room. As she entered the room, the calmest feeling came over her. When she looked in the crib, Zack was sleeping peacefully. With gratitude in her heart, Meggan kissed Zack on the cheek, flipped off the light, and left the room, knowing that it wasn't just Zack who was being tended and watched over on that dark night.

In Greek, the word for *Comforter* means "advocate" or "one who is summoned to the side of another to strengthen and support in times of distress and danger." Heavenly Father will send the Comforter, the Holy Ghost. Don't do life alone. There is no joy in that. Rather, draw near unto Him and He will draw near unto you, and you will know the peace, the comfort that passes all understanding.

From an experience related by Meggan Arave.

To Whom Shall We Go?

It's hard for some to accept, but nonetheless it's true that we live in trying times, and if our commitment to Christian discipleship is lukewarm, we will not weather the storms ahead. Considering this sobering fact, there is a story in John 6 that inspires me, especially when the tests and trials seem too much for me to bear.

Two and one-half years into His ministry, Jesus was at the height of His popularity. Literally thousands followed Him and sought to hear Him or see His miracles. Late one afternoon, Jesus miraculously fed more than five thousand men, along with women and children, with five loaves and two small fishes—a great miracle. So impressed were the people by this miracle that they attempted to force Jesus to be king. Jesus, of course, would have none of it.

The next day they came looking for Him again, hoping again to be fed by Him. Jesus rebuked them. They could think no further than their bellies. He commanded them to "Labour not for the meat which perisheth, but for that meat which endureth unto everlasting life" (John 6:27)—to which they replied, "Lord, evermore give us this bread. And Jesus said unto them, I am the bread of life" (John 6:34–35).

And indeed, He is. He is the staff of our eternal life, the only and true source of spiritual sustenance, and they knew it. They knew what He meant and what He was claiming, and they were offended by His words and began to murmur.

Jesus rebuked them for murmuring, and He continued by teaching that without Him, not one of them would have claim on eternal life.

That really offended them. Sitting in that Capernaum synagogue were not only a host of the curious and the skeptics, but also a significant crowd of His disciples. And they too were offended by His strong doctrine—so much and so many, in fact, that it is recorded, "From that time many of His disciples went back and walked no more with him" (John 6:66). The test was just too much.

Well, as they walked away—and can you visualize this?—Jesus turned to the Twelve and said, "Will ye also go away?" (John 6:67).

And Peter answered on behalf of the Twelve—and I love his answer—"Lord, to whom shall we go? thou hast the words of eternal life. And we believe and are sure that thou art the Christ, the Son of the living God" (John 6:68–69).

These were not fair-weather followers. To them it was Him, and only Him. No test, no trial would turn them away.

May it be so with us. When we are tested and tried, and when others tempt us to turn our backs and walk away, may we look to the Savior with steeled resolve and singleness of heart, and say similarly, "Lord, to whom shall we go?" (John 6:68).

Adapted from John 6.

Misti's Balloon

The Savior once said, "Ask, and ye shall receive, seek and ye shall find, knock and it shall be opened unto you" (D&C 88:63). It interests me that each of those words keynotes effort.

I want you to know that prayer works, and nothing is so trivial or insignificant that we cannot counsel with the Lord about it. I have a friend who years ago learned this important principle.

When she was just seven years old, she went to the fair with her brother. They both came home with helium-filled balloons. Misti took hers outside to play. Well, you can probably guess what happened. It wasn't long before she let go of the string, and her balloon floated away. Disappointed, she went inside and told her mom.

Mom told her not to take her brother's balloon outside because it might also get lost. Again, you can probably guess what happened. Misti grabbed her brother's balloon and out the door she went with a promise that she wouldn't lose it.

Fewer than ten minutes later, however, she let go of it, and this time the balloon floated up to the top of a tall tree, where it got stuck. In tears, Misti went inside to tell Mom. Mom came out, took one look, and told Misti there was no way they were going to be able to get that balloon down.

Crying and scared that her brother would be mad, Misti then did what good parents had taught her to do. She knelt down right there in the grass next to the tree, and in the tender innocence of a seven-year-old girl, pleaded with Heavenly Father to help her get the balloon back. She closed the prayer, opened her eyes, and looked up just in time to see that balloon float right down into her hand.

Misti stopped crying. Excited and filled with the sweet assurance of knowing that her prayer had been heard, she ran inside to tell Mom. As she poured out her heart to Mom, Mom didn't say a word. She just stood there and cried.

I believe that when we are sincerely trying to be good, no matter what it is, if it's important to us, it's important to Him.

Adapted from an experience of Misti Lyn Archibald.

o

JAIRUS

On one occasion as the Master beached a small boat near Capernaum, He was met by Jairus, the ruler of the synagogue in Capernaum. Jairus's twelve-year-old daughter was dying. We're not told why, only that the onward roll of nature that brings death eventually to us all was nigh to claiming this daughter so dearly loved by her father. Desperate to stay nature's course, Jairus asks the Master to intercede, saying, "My little daughter lieth at the point of death: I pray thee, come and lay thy hands on her . . . and she shall live" (Mark 5:23).

Recognizing that this was real faith, Jesus went with Jairus. While en route, however, they were met by messengers from Jairus's house announcing to him that which he least wanted to hear—his daughter had died. Overhearing that dread declaration, Jesus bolstered the grieving father's faith. "Be not afraid," He said, "only believe" (Mark 5:36).

When they arrived at the house, Jesus excused the paid professional mourners who scorned Him, whose noise was an irksome disruption to the Spirit of the Lord. Then, taking with Him only Peter, James, and John and the damsel's parents, Jesus entered the death chamber. Can you imagine being one of those parents and the hope you would have burning inside you that Jesus can help?

Taking the girl by the hand, He said, "Damsel, I say unto thee, arise!" (Mark 5:41).

And immediately she arose; even more, she walked. Again, I can only imagine the inexpressible joy of those parents, and I think I can imagine a warm, tender smile on the face of the Master as He witnessed this joyful reunion. After swearing them to secrecy that they tell no man of the miracle, Jesus commanded them that they should feed this daughter and restore her bodily strength.

I love this story. It's beautiful. My thoughts to you come more in the form of a question than a statement. I wonder how many times nature has dictated a disaster to befall our loved ones, and it has been averted because you and I prayed and called down the powers of a loving God—and He interceded and saved them. How many priceless blessings have you and I received in such a manner and never knew we had? I guess I'm just simple-minded enough to believe that this has happened many times for you and for me. I would hope that we would never underestimate the power of prayer for those we love, that we would never stop praying for them, and that we will thereby place our loved ones under the umbrella of a loving God's care each day.

Samaritan Woman

Early in the Savior's ministry, He took occasion to travel from Judea to Galilee by way of Samaria. Most Jews at that time considered a Samaritan the lowest class of human being on the earth, and Jews would not associate with Samaritans—would not even travel through their land. But Jesus, pressed by a need unknown to us, journeyed on the forbidden soil.

Around noon, Jesus and the Twelve stop near Jacob's well in the land of the Samaritans. It's hot, and Jesus is tired. As the disciples go away to buy food, Jesus rests on the edge of the well. A woman approaches the well carrying a water pot.

Jesus says to her, "Give me to drink" (John 4:7).

Recognizing that He's a Jew, the woman is shocked that He has broken custom and even spoken to her.

"How is it," she inquires, "that thou, being a Jew, askest drink of me, which am a woman of Samaria?" (John 4:9).

It seems right here that Jesus sets aside His thirst momentarily and focuses on the woman and the teaching opportunity afforded Him. He replies, "If thou knewest the gift of God, and who it is that saith to thee, Give me to drink; thou wouldest have asked of him, and he would have given thee living water" (John 4:10).

The woman doesn't understand. She's thinking literally about water and water pots, but the Master is speaking figuratively. So, patiently and gently, Jesus leads her to a point of spiritual readiness where she is now prepared to be taught the gospel.

Then Jesus abruptly says to her, "Go, call thy husband, and come hither" (John 4:16).

The woman replies in shamed truth, "I have no husband" (John 4:17).

And now perhaps we see why she is coming to draw water in the heat of the day when there's no other person at the well, because Jesus says, "Thou hast well said, I have no husband: For thou hast had five husbands; and he whom thou now hast is not thy husband: in that saidst thou truly" (John 4:17–18).

I love this part of the story. This woman was grossly unworthy. Her life has been one of poor choices and many mistakes, yet does the Master turn away? Does He deny her or deem her unworthy of His help? No! In fact, in bold and undeniable terms, He declares to her, in one of those rare instances that He did so, that He is the promised Messiah.

So impressed and converted is this woman that because of her, many Samaritan souls come out to hear Jesus, and they too are converted.

I conclude from this story that I don't need to reach a certain level of worthiness to receive help from my Savior. That's why He's the Savior: He can save me—anytime, anywhere, and in any pitiful condition I'm in—if I'm willing to be helped. If you stop and think about what we want to be and where we want to be and what we are at the present time, none of us is worthy and never will be without Him—but He still loves us.

Adapted from John 4.

Skiing Faith

On a recent cross-country skiing vacation, I learned a meaningful lesson about, of all things, faith.

We got to our rustic cabin late in the day. After unpacking, several of us decided we wanted to go out for a skiing run, even if it was late. According to the map, there was a trail not too far from our cabin that was a two-and-a-half-mile loop. We strapped on our skis, and off we went.

Well, it got dark a lot faster than we had anticipated. By the time we were a mile or so along that trail, it was so dark we couldn't see the snow in front of us; we couldn't even see the trail directly under our feet. It became very difficult to ski. The more I tried to pick out the trail, the more difficulty I had.

By then, we were deep into the pine forests of Island Park. Every tree looked the same. That trail had twisted and turned and gone up and down and around in every way imaginable. None of us was totally sure of which way was home. The temperature was dropping close to zero. In short, this was not a good place, nor a good night, in which to get lost.

Then all of a sudden it dawned on me. We were on a groomed trail. All we had to do was relax, keep our skis in the tracks of those who had gone before us, and simply follow them home. With that newfound knowledge, it became much easier to ski. I stopped worrying about where to steer my skis, and I just let the trail guide me. Calmer now, I began to look around. The snow was beautiful. The stars overhead were bright and beautiful; it was a gorgeous, clear, crisp, mountain night.

We skied on in the dark, more or less blind. Then suddenly, we broke out of the trees onto the banks of the Buffalo River. I knew exactly where we were. The lights of our little cabin were just a short distance downstream. We skied on, and in due time arrived back to the warmth and security of our cabin and the rest of the family. What could have been a disaster became instead an exhilarating and a joyful experience.

Life is a lot like a ski trip. It begins as the grandest of adventures. But there inevitably come those times, I think for all of us, when we feel like we're lost in the woods, skiing blind in the dark. There are some even now, especially among the young, who don't know where they are, or even who they are. They are lost skiing in spiritual darkness, if you will. I remember that feeling; I remember it well!

My dear friends, life is a short loop. We came from the warmth of God's presence into a cold, darkened world. And a trail has been laid out clearly before us that will lead us back to Him and to His love. The real test of this life is whether we will trust the trail at all times. Are we willing to humbly place our faith in the ones who have gone before us?

Just because you can't see the trail clearly or the end from the beginning does not mean that the trail's not there. Don't abandon the Lord's trail! There is none of us who has learned enough to make it home on our own. Stay in the tracks, even when all hell is trying to pull you off and get you as lost as they are.

I promise you that if you do, the day will come when the light will appear before you, and you will the know the unspeakable joy reserved for those who endure to the end.

The Weight Set

One evening I was in the kitchen preparing dinner. My son Jed approached me and started to say something. Then he stopped, grinned at me, and said, "Nah, never mind." And he turned and walked away, leaving me standing there wondering.

Well, a short time later, I heard this plaintive cry coming from the direction of the basement: "Dad!"

It was Jed. It didn't sound too desperate and I was busy, so I ignored it.

A few seconds later it came again: "Dad!"

"What?" I hollered back.

There was no answer, so I went back to work.

A few seconds later, "Dad!"

There was a little more urgency in his voice now.

"What do you want?" I asked.

There was no response. Then, a second or two later, it came again: "Dad!"

Now he sounded desperate. This made no sense. So, I finally went downstairs to see what was going on, and when I got to the bottom of the stairs, there was my son lying on his weight bench with a weighted barbell across his chest. His face was turning red. It didn't take me long to figure out what had happened.

A few days before, he had approached me wanting to "max out on weight," as he called it, which meant that he wanted to lift more than he'd ever done before. I warned him not to do that.

Now here he was, pinned flat on his back, his face beet-red, unable to move. Sure enough, he had loaded up the bar, laid down on the bench, and lifted it off. Down it had come, flat onto his chest! He was unable, try as he might, to get it back up.

I could see that he was in no immediate danger. I started laughing.

"I ought to just leave you here," I said.

"No!" he cried in desperation.

Since I had a captive audience, I figured that a teaching moment was in order. I asked him if he'd learned anything.

Emphatically he nodded his head, "Yes—ah, yes!"

I took pity on him, and I lifted the weights off.

But you know, the more I thought about that, there is something about that experience that seems hauntingly familiar. I don't know how many times in my life I have overestimated my abilities, underestimated life, and wound up spiritually and emotionally pinned, out of breath, with the world on my chest.

I am so grateful that I am God's son. He lets me try, and He has always come to my rescue when it was too much for me. And you know, I don't ever remember Him laughing at me or threatening me as He set me free, but set me free He has always done.

Hezekiah's Test

"Be strong and courageous, be not afraid nor dismayed . . . for there be more with us than with him" (2 Chronicles 32:7). I like those words. So spoke Hezekiah, king of Judah, in the day that the Assyrian army entered his land and began conquering the outlying towns and villages. Hezekiah worked desperately to prepare his people against the most powerful army on the face of the earth. But what could he do?

Let me tell you a little about Hezekiah.

Hezekiah was one of Judah's most righteous kings. He not only kept the commandments of God more faithfully than any king before or after him, but he persuaded his people to do the same. To an apostate Jewish nation, he brought faith, joy, and prosperity once more. But now everything was threatened by Assyria.

Sennacherib, the Assyrian king, even sent to Jerusalem messengers who stood on the wall before the people and said to them, "Let not Hezekiah deceive you: for he shall not be able to deliver you out of my hand: Neither let Hezekiah make you trust in the Lord" (2 Kings 18:29–30). "Hearken not to Hezekiah" (2 Kings 18:31).

The Assyrian army then moved up, and almost 200,000 men surrounded Jerusalem.

Even though Isaiah, the great prophet, had assured Hezekiah that the city would not fall, still, consider this situation. The odds are incalculable—Hezekiah's pitiful band of farmers, women, and children armed with darts and shields against the mightiest army on earth surrounding them on every side. Hezekiah has on one hand the simple promise of deliverance by God's prophet stacked against

200,000 men and the open and avowed hostility of the mightiest nation on earth. Do you see the test?

What God has promised looks absolutely impossible in the face of the opposition. Is it any wonder that Hezekiah humbles himself, bows before the Lord, and enters the temple to pray, saying, "O Lord our God, save us from his hand, that all the kingdoms of the Earth may know that thou art the Lord, even thou only" (Isaiah 37:20)?

In response to this humble and sweet prayer, the Lord sends Isaiah, the prophet, with this assurance: "[Sennacherib] shall not come into this city, nor even shoot an arrow there. . . . By the way that he came, by the same shall he return . . . saith the Lord" (2 Kings 19:32–33).

That night, as Judah prayed and Assyria slept, the angel of the Lord entered the Assyrian camp, and the next morning 185,000 Assyrian soldiers lay dead upon the ground around Jerusalem. Those still alive ran for home. The Lord's promises were fulfilled in every detail.

The faithful will always be tested. Why? How else can they lay down in deeds done the intents of their hearts? It's not enough to want to be good. We must prove ourselves good. How can the faithful ever know their strength or the Lord's strength unless they are given the opportunity under stress to discover both?

Further, when the opposition and the obstacles make the promises of the Lord seem impossible, remember, "Be strong . . . be not afraid . . . for there be more with us than with him" (2 Chronicles 32:7).

Buried by the Wayside

In the summer of 1864, Jesse Nathaniel Smith was returning to his family from a mission in Denmark. At the Missouri River in Nebraska, he joined with a company of emigrants, mostly women and children, bound for Zion in what were called "down and back wagon trains." It was a particularly difficult year for the emigrants with much death and disease along the trail—much of it due to cholera. Jesse wrote the following:

>One sultry noon, as soon as the halt was made the word went around that a young sister had died during the morning drive and would be buried immediately. The preparations for the solemnity were of the simplest character. While the men dug the grave a short distance away upon a low bench or plateaus, the women wrapped the form of the deceased in many folds of blankets. There was no bier, and the body was somewhat rudely, though tenderly borne to the place of sepulcher by friendly hands. And what had been her history, we eagerly enquired. The short story of her life was soon told. She had been for years a member of the church in England, and for a considerable time betrothed to a young missionary who could not well be spared to emigrate. They had agreed that they would not get married until he should be released, and then they would make the journey together. They were married on board the ship, but a few short weeks had passed, and now her dream of married life and earthly happiness was over. The young husband was too ill to follow the burial party without assistance. His grief was very touching. Green boughs and young willows and a profusion of

wildflowers formed the only substitute for a coffin. As we looked down into the grave, it seemed hard to leave her there alone, amid that sea of waving grass, in that unmarked spot—but our reflections were abruptly interrupted by the captain's hoarse voice calling to the guard to drive in the cattle.

Once again, it is good to occasionally be reminded of how far we have come and on whose shoulders we stand.

Source: https://history.churchofjesuschrist.org/overlandtravel/sources/39729307348073711210-eng/j-n-s-jesse-n-smith-buried-by-the-wayside-juvenile-instructor-17-jan-1874-14?firstName=Jesse%20Nathaniel&surname=Smith

The Red Flake

A couple of years ago I went with some friends to climb the Grand Teton in Wyoming. It was one of the grandest adventures of my life.

On the morning of the second day as we began the actual ascent of the Grand itself, we came to a place in our route that was called "the Red Flake." Up to this point in the climb, it had been pretty much just a steep, no-risk hike up the hill. But that all changed right here. The Red Flake was a ledge on a rock wall about two and a half feet long by six to eight inches wide with an outcropping of rock jutting straight up from the ledge. The trail went over that ledge, and there was no way around it—at least none that I knew of. In order to cross the ledge, I had to turn my face toward the rock wall, hug the outcropping that was sticking up, and scoot my feet side to side across the ledge.

What's the big deal about a little ol' ledge? Well, while my toes were up against the wall, my heels and backside were hanging out into thin air. I don't remember how far down it was, but I do remember that it was far enough down that when I first stepped up and looked over, my blood pressure went into orbit. I wasn't about to turn around at that point and go back and look like a coward. So I hugged that outcropping like it was my mother. Without looking down or breathing, I scooted across.

Once I got across, I felt a great feeling of accomplishment, like I had faced my fears and defeated them. I probably shouldn't say it, but I was proud of myself. I thought, *Ah, that wasn't so bad.* And you know, it turned out that it wasn't so bad, compared to some of the other climbs we got into later that day. But I have to say, all things considered, it was worth it, because the higher we climbed that day, the more incredible the view and the more awesome became the experience, until finally that afternoon, it climaxed as we stood at the summit.

I'll never forget the momentary feeling of dizziness I felt when I raised myself up to full height at 14,000 feet. It was a little bit like standing on top of a tall stepladder. There was nothing above me and nothing to hang on to. It was one of the headiest experiences I've ever had. Oh, and the view—there's no way to describe it. I aimed my camera and turned 360 degrees, snapping pictures continuously. But those pictures don't even begin to do it justice. I guess it was a little bit like I was seeing things more the way God does. I could see so much and so far, and it was all so clear. I don't hesitate to say I've never been the same since that experience.

But you know, if I hadn't crossed the Red Flake, I would have missed all of it, and worse yet, I would never have even known what I missed.

In my lifetime, I've read the scriptures a bit, and I've come to realize that the scriptures themselves, and especially books like Isaiah, are like the Red Flake. They are something of a rite of passage, if you will. As we muster the determination and the courage to face them and conquer them, grander and grander vistas will be opened to our view, and the hope of the summit will burn brighter and brighter to light our way.

Indeed, great are the words of Isaiah, and they are a rite of passage, because they will lead us to that grandest of all summits: to look upon the face of our Redeemer, to see His smile of favor upon us, and to be welcomed into His presence.

Obedience Always

What is the purpose of life? Of the many things that you have to get done today, which is the most important? To every Christian, this story reveals the answer.

One day, while Jesus was on the road, a young man came running after Him. Upon reaching the Master, the man knelt at His feet and asked, "Good Master, what good thing shall I do that I may have eternal life?" (Matthew 19:16).

Jesus responded to Him the same as He had earlier done with the lawyer; He referred him to the scriptures. "Keep th commandments," He said. "Do not commit adultery, do not kill, do not steal, do not bear false witness, defraud not, honour thy father and mother" (Mark 10:19).

Whereupon the man asked, "Master, all these things have I kept from my youth up; What lack I yet?" (Matthew 19:20).

How many of us, like this man, have gone charging after the Lord filled with zeal and momentary enthusiasm, only to wander away later when something else caught our attention? I cannot recall how many times I have prayed with all my heart for help and answers and then paid little attention when they came.

May it be understood that it is one thing to come unto the Lord, but it is another to follow Him thereafter. Any man who asks the Lord for revelation had better be prepared to obey it when it comes, or he is worse off than if he had never asked.

Jesus loved the rich young ruler, and, out of respect for his agency, gave him what he asked for. He wanted a great thing revealed, and it was.

"One thing thou lackest:" the Savior said, "go thy way, sell whatsoever thou hast, and give to the poor, and thou shalt have treasure in heaven: and come, take up the cross, and follow me" (Mark 10:21).

The young man "was sad at that saying, and went away grieved; for he had great possessions" (Mark 10:22).

I wish this story was a parable, but it is not. It is history that I fear continually repeats itself. Obedience is the first law of heaven and the foremost duty of man. The sum of our existence, the only source of our joy, is to find the truth and obey it.

What then is the most important thing you can do today? Find out exactly what the Lord wants and obey the same way.

Joshua and the Spies

The children of Israel had been out of Egypt only a few months when Moses gathered twelve men and sent them as spies into the land of Canaan. They were to "see the land" (Numbers 13:18) and bring back a report. They were also told to bring back some of its fruit. Moses told them, "be ye of good courage" (Numbers 13: 20).

They were gone for forty days, and they traveled the length of the land. When they returned, they stood before Moses and all Israel to make their report. They carried a cluster of grapes so large that it had to be carried between two men on a staff. That's a lot of grapes. "[T]he land" they said, "floweth with milk and honey" (Numbers 13:27).

But then ten of the spies turned their description to that which had most caught their attention: the present inhabitants of Canaan. In an exaggerated fashion, they told of great walled cities and of giants before whom they were as grasshoppers. "[T]hey are stronger then we," was their cowardly conclusion (Numbers 13:31).

But two of the spies, Joshua and Caleb, were filled with a different spirit. With faith, they "stilled the people . . . and said, Let us go up at once, and possess it; for we are well able to overcome it" (Numbers 13:30).

Unfortunately, the children of Israel believed the report of doom and gloom, and they wept all that night. The next day they arose and appointed a new leader and prepared to return to Egypt.

Caleb and Joshua "rent their clothes" (Numbers 14:6) and with great courage stood before the people of Israel and pled with them to have faith in their God and "rebel not" (Numbers 14:9). In reply to their pleadings, the people sought to "stone them" (Numbers 14:10).

The Lord intervened and saved Caleb and Joshua, but Israel—and especially the weak-hearted spies—were cursed. For every day the spies searched Canaan, Israel would wander one year in the wilderness, until all of that generation were dead. Only the children that faithless Israel said would be a prey to their enemies would be privileged to inherit the rich land. And so it was fulfilled.

Is it any different now? We are striving for a promised land that flows with milk and honey. Yet there are those among us who lack vision and see only the obstacles and dangers along the way. Continually we are bombarded by the negative and inundated by the gloom. It's enough to depress a person.

This is wrong! We are the children of God, and He has the power to see us through. To focus on the negative is like unto doing the evil. Both come naturally; they are the easy way, and they are of the evil one. Yes, we need to be aware of the obstacles, but we need to be focused with faith on their conquering.

This is pleasing to the Lord. As we are obedient to Him, there is no need to worry and be afraid of anything

I close with Joshua's inspired words: "Be strong and of a good courage" (Joshua 1:6).

Be not afraid.

Adapted from Numbers 13–14.

Sweet-and-Sour Rice

My wife and I had been married only a few months, and she was expecting our first child. I was an overloaded university student, and she was working full time. It was that awful stage of the pregnancy called "morning sickness," which is a nice way of saying that she was sick morning, noon, and night—all the time. Even the sight and smell of food was a traumatic experience for her.

One evening I got home before she did, and since I love my wife, I decided to make supper so she wouldn't have to. I pondered on what to fix. I really wanted it to be good. I inventoried the kitchen, which eliminated many things I wanted to fix. Then I inventoried what I knew how to fix, and that eliminated almost everything else that was edible. I did manage, however, to find some rice, and I decided to make sweet-and-sour rice. That had always been one of my favorites. The problem was I had never prepared sweet-and-sour rice, nor ever seen it done—and what's more, I didn't have a recipe.

Nah, I thought, *how hard can it be?* I went to work and boiled the rice. But then I wondered, *how can you make rice sweet and sour at the same time?* Well, I couldn't think of any magical ingredient that would do it, so I took the name literally: Sweet-and-Sour Rice. I hunted in the cupboard and I found something sweet—ha, sugar! I poured a generous amount of sugar into the rice. Now I needed something sour—hmm, aw, lemon juice! I found some lemon juice in the refrigerator and I poured it in. When I stirred it all together, it didn't look quite like the sweet-and-sour rice that I'd eaten in restaurants. Yeah, it still needed something.

My mother taught me that you always make a meal balanced. Well, the only thing I could think of to balance the meal was a vegetable. I hunted around in our meager stock, and I found some canned peas. And since there was no sense in dirtying any more dishes, I dumped the peas in with the rice, and I stirred it all together. My creation was complete: Sweet-and-Sour Rice with Peas, overcooked.

At this point, I have to be honest. I looked at what I had created, and I didn't have the stomach to eat it. I left the masterpiece on the stove simmering with a note and went back to campus and ate. When Debbie came home, she read my note and bravely sat down to eat that rice. To this day, I have considered it a selfless act of love and courage that she even attempted to eat that mess. It should have been used to patch cracks in the sidewalk or something.

I have heard it said that "men are from Mars and women are from Venus." Well, I don't know about that. I think they both come from heaven, and I think that God makes them deliberately different so that the eternity they spend understanding each other and becoming one makes them one with God at the same time. Please don't forget: Marriage is a man, a woman, and a God.

The Tree of Life

This year as you decorate your Christmas tree, I have a story I'd like you to think about. There's a great mystery in the Holy Bible. Our first parents, Adam and Eve, partook of the forbidden fruit, and thereby became mortal. You remember the story. The opportunity for man to be and become began then.

However, here's the mystery: There were two trees in the Garden of Eden: the tree of knowledge of good and evil and the tree of life.

After partaking of the forbidden fruit, Adam and Eve were cast out of the garden and were not allowed to return and partake of the tree of life. And from there, it seems as though the entire Bible is a saga of man's continued fall from that mysterious tree. What was that tree, and how do we get back to it?

Thirty-four centuries later, another great prophet saw that same tree of life in a vision. He described the fruit of that tree as beautiful, white, and precious above every other fruit. And, of course, he wanted to know what the tree meant.

In response to his question, he was shown in vision the most beautiful woman he had ever seen. It was Mary, the mother of Jesus, who would not be born for some six hundred years. The next thing he saw was Mary caught away in the Spirit of the Lord, and when he next saw her, she was bearing the Christ child in her arms.

After witnessing the scenes of Christmas, the prophet was then asked if he now understood the meaning of the tree of life.

"Yea," he said in answer, "it is the love of God, which sheddeth itself abroad in the hearts of the children of men" (1 Nephi 11:22).

The tree of life was a representation of God's love, and Christ's birth was the gift given to us of that love. Thus, Christmas is all about man's return to the tree of love. Christ came to lead us back to the love of God. There is nothing in this world that is more powerful, more pure, more precious, and more desirable than to partake of the love of almighty God through Jesus Christ. That love is so powerful, it is life itself. To have that love, to feel that love is to live, and to live without that love is to no more than exist.

Now, do you understand? Christmas has always been, and still is, all about love—God for His Son, the Son for us, and us for each other. This year, this Christmas, I hope that the gift of charity, that perfect, pure, and unfailing love, may take root in your heart and become a tree of life that reaches toward heaven and spreads over your family and friends.

You know, now that I think about it, somehow it seems fitting that the symbol at the center of our Christmas is an evergreen tree.

The Dirt on the Road

It must have been a curious sight that day to see city workers scattering loads of dirt in the street.

Normally those men labored to keep their prospering city clean and free of mud and filth, but there they were—out spreading load after load of good, old-fashioned dirt on the cobblestone streets, right in front of one of the most prominent buildings in the largest city in the United States.

It's not surprising that history has all but forgotten that misplaced soil. But there's a lesson there.

The location of that dirt was Sixth and Chestnut streets in Philadelphia, Pennsylvania. The building was the venerable old Pennsylvania Statehouse, which you would know as Independence Hall, where the Declaration of Independence had once been debated and signed. The date on which that dirt was being scattered in front of that building was May 14, 1787. Philadelphia, and the entire nation for that matter, had their eyes anxiously fixed on that building. Why? Because on that day, some of America's best men were slated to convene and save the freedom won by the Revolution.

So, why the dirt? Silence. It was there to muffle distracting noise of horse hooves and clatter of carriage wheels over hard cobblestones. Just a few feet away from that street, those men would scour the wisdom of the centuries to form a new government. History would come to call that gathering the Grand Convention.

Someone understood that inspiration is invited by peace and stillness. Revelation comes when good men gather in council wrestling with righteous problems seeking heaven's help. And oh, how those men struggled! But it came. Praise be to God, inspiration came. The Constitution of the United States is the most powerful document of human law outside the cannon of scripture—it is scripture!—because God gave good men revelation, sometimes in spite of themselves, to capture anew eternal principles. It was a document born in council, and foreordained, its principles and its officers bound by oath to preserve the rights and liberties of all men.

They That Be with Us

I would like to share one of the first Old Testament stories that ever impressed me as a child. In that story, it seems that the king of Syria declared war on Israel. But every time he attempted to ambush the king of Israel, Elisha, the prophet of God, would warn Israel's king, and the ambush would be thwarted.

This happened so many times that the Syrian king became convinced he had spies somewhere in his ranks who were tipping off Israel's king.

A servant of the Syrian king told him that Elisha the prophet was the one warning Israel's king. The king of Syria then determined that he was going to take Elisha.

Through spies, he learned that Elisha was staying in Dothan. The king sent a large army of men with chariots and horses, and by night they surrounded the city of Dothan. Early the next morning, Elisha's servant came outside, and what did he see? An army of Syrian soldiers surrounding the city. Imagine waking up to that! In a panic, he ran back to Elisha.

He asks Elisha what they are going to do (see 2 Kings 6:15).

I think I know in part a little of how he must have felt. I don't know how many times in recent years I have been surrounded and overwhelmed with opposition, responsibility, and deadlines. There have been times when I could see absolutely no way out, and I, too, was in a worried panic. And I suspect I'm probably not the only one who's been there. If you're there now, or soon will be, this is the rest of the story.

Elisha came out and surveyed the situation. "Fear not:" he said, "for they that be with us are more than they that be with them" (2 Kings 6:16).

I almost laugh when I think of the reaction of Elisha's servant to that. Surely he could count, couldn't he? Just imagine the look on his face when he counted two against an entire army!

Elisha knew that his servant didn't understand, so he prayed, "Lord I pray thee, open his eyes, that he may see" (2 Kings 6:17).

Suddenly, the eyes of Elisha's servant were opened, and he saw on the mountains around the city a great heavenly host with fiery horses and chariots surrounding the Syrian army and standing in protection of the man of God.

Even though the record is silent, I believe the servant of Elisha had a great boost to his confidence with that and was no longer worried (see 2 Kings 6).

Nor should we be!

We live in the presence of the hosts of heaven. They see us, they know us, and they love us, and oft times in difficult situations are appointed to help us, though we may never see them.

The Savior once said, "Be still, and know that I am God" (Psalms 46:10).

May the Lord so bless you.

The Garbage Truck Driver

Someone once said, "What ere thou art, act well thy part." Now, what a true and profound statement!

One morning as I was fixing breakfast, the garbage truck started down my street. I remembered that my garbage can was full and that I had forgotten to put it out. I asked my son to hurry and get it to the curb. Now at the time, he was not very big, and the can outweighed him. In his frantic efforts to beat the truck, he tipped the can over, spilling garbage everywhere.

A few minutes later I came to the window to see if he had made it, and I saw the disgusting mess. It was then that I noticed with some interest that the garbage truck was stopped in front of my house, idling. I went out to investigate. I was surprised to discover the driver of the truck had gotten out of the truck and was helping my son clean up the mess. As I approached, I fully expected the man to be less than pleased at having his busy schedule delayed and having to pick up my smelly garbage. However, with garbage in his hands, he smiled warmly and greeted me cheerfully. After the exchange of a few pleasantries, he climbed back in his truck, emptied my can, and drove off with a smile and a wave.

Ever after that, when I saw that man driving that garbage truck, he was always sporting a smile and a cheerful countenance, and more often than not, he waved to me. I found myself going out of my way to wave to him, and even to place my can where it would be easier for him to pick up. I never met a man driving a garbage truck who seemed to love life more, who was more cheerful and who impressed me more.

Maybe life hasn't handed you and me the most favorable set of circumstances, but does that mean we can't love life or be of good cheer? Absolutely not! If we are to bloom where we are planted, and I assure you we are, may it be as a beautiful flower, and not as a stinky weed.

Abraham's Test

Not long ago I watched one of my daughters struggle in learning to play the piano. She had developed a habit in her playing that would severely inhibit her ability to learn new music and eventually master the instrument. I watched as her teacher coaxed and pleaded to talk her out of this habit, but my daughter resisted. She could see no sense in giving up her technique when the new technique only seemed a difficult waste of time. After all, she figured, she could play songs, couldn't she?

In the Old Testament, there is a philosophically challenging story. All his life, Abraham had wanted a son, and finally in his old age, miraculously that covenant son Isaac was born. Abraham rejoiced in his birth.

Then came the day when the voice of the Lord commanded Abraham to "Take now thy son, thine only son Isaac, whom thou lovest, and get thee into the land of Moriah; and offer him [up] there for a burnt offering upon one of the mountains which I will [shall] tell thee of" (Genesis 22:2).

Without a hint of procrastination, Abraham rose early the next morning and made his way to the mount. There he built the altar, laid the wood, placed Isaac on it, and stretched forth the knife to kill him.

Now, at first glance this command of God seems cruel and illogical. Why would God ask such a thing, especially since His promises to Abraham concerning posterity depended entirely on Isaac? Could God have asked of a father anything more difficult than to kill his long-awaited son, a son for whom Abraham had such a love that even God mentions it? And to ask such a thing would have been especially repugnant to Abraham, who himself had once been laid on an altar and nearly sacrificed because of his idolatrous father.

Why, then, does God ask? Is He testing this man, who has already given his all, just to test him? Is there something an omniscient God wants to learn about Abraham? No! No, such a thought is ridiculous!

The angel then commanded Abraham not to kill his son, saying, "now I know that thou fearest God, seeing thou hast not withheld thy son, thine only son from me" (Genesis 22:12).

To me, the key word is *withheld*. God has designed to crown each of us with more glory, honor, and power than we can possibly comprehend at the present time. But He can do this only if we are willing to trust Him completely and not withhold anything from Him. How can we be the master, lest we first be the student—and a willing one at that?

Abraham's quick obedience brought forth a quick response from heaven, and Abraham's joy and faith became as great as was his pain moments earlier.

May each of us be as our ancient father, withholding nothing from God now so that later He will withhold nothing from us.

"Can You See What I Just Did to You?"

Sometimes it was a struggle to get the students in seminary to do an entire devotional, so when one of Brother Kenley's students at Granger High School asked to do the whole thing, he was overjoyed. But then the young man said, "I will be using a guitar."

"Okay," Brother Kenley said.

"I will be using an electric guitar," the student explained.

"Okaaay!" Brother Kenley said.

"And it will be amplified," the boy concluded. When Brother Kenley asked how loud it would be, the boy responded, **"Loud!"**

That familiar voice said, "let him do it," so Brother Kenley gave him the go-ahead. His next thought was that he should warn the other teachers. Brother Kenley explains what followed.

> The day came. He had everything set up and ready to go. I stood in the back of my classroom waiting. His first song was so beautiful I thought I was going to cry and, as I looked around the room, I saw others completely involved. His second song was a bit more animated and there was a lot of toe tapping going on in the room with a ton of smiles. Then came the third song. A really loud head banger that about brought bricks out of the wall. I was even jerking my head in time with the music. All of a sudden, he turned that amplified sound into dead silence about half-way through the song. Students who had been almost bouncing out of their desks were almost angrily hollering for him to keep going. Quietly, he turned, put his guitar away and turned to the class and said, "Can you see what I just did to you with music in a few short minutes? What can Satan do to us

with music if we aren't very careful?" He quietly sat down at his desk to a very quiet and pensive room full of students—which included me.

This boy well understood the power of music and entertainment. As President Russell M. Nelson said, "Each time we resist entertainment or ideologies that celebrate covenant-breaking, we are exercising faith in Him, which in turn increases our faith" ("Embrace the Future with Faith," General Conference, October 2020).

Source: Personal experience of Lynn Kenley.

Powerful Contradictions

When life's ironies hurt, when our expectations are cruelly crushed, and when those we most trust deal us the deepest pain, would you remember this about the Lord Jesus Christ?

In His life, Jesus was exposed to greater contradictions than any who ever lived. Life gave Him more disappointments and more cruel ironies than any mortal could have ever born. So much was the Savior's life a study in irony that Isaiah devoted an entire chapter to it (see Isaiah 53).

Isaiah said, "he hath no form nor comeliness; and when we see him there is no beauty that we should desire him" (Isaiah 53:2).

Wouldn't you expect that the Son of God would have looked like a God? It was not so. Jesus appeared a normal man. No man ever born who appeared so ordinary was given a greater genetic endowment.

"He is despised," Isaiah continued, "and rejected of men" (Isaiah 53:3).

Family, friends, and neighbors—those who should have loved the Savior—were those who turned the coldest hearts to Him. Oh, how this must have hurt! No man ever born who more deserved to be welcomed and revered was more universally hated and ill-treated.

Remember the words, "a man of sorrows, and acquainted with grief" (Isaiah 53:3)?

Righteousness, my friends, is not a guarantee of peace and happiness. The truth is, the better we do, the more trial mortality will give us. After all, He who had the greatest power by perfection to live happily experienced the deepest anguish.

Isaiah wrote, "he hath borne our griefs, and carried our sorrows: yet we did esteem him stricken, smitten of God, and afflicted" (Isaiah 53:4).

While Jesus carried mankind to the safety of God's arms, He was reviled by those He saved and considered as cursed by the very God He served. While they carried Him to the cross, He carried us. As the cross bore Him unto death, He bore us unto life. Never were more thanks deserved when less was given.

"[H]e was bruised for our iniquities: the chastisement of our peace was upon him: and with his stripes we are healed" (Isaiah 53:5).

There never lived a man less deserving of punishment who was more punished than He. His hurt, my friend, was your healing. That's an irony.

"[T]he Lord laid on him the iniquity of us all" (Isaiah 53:6).

Jesus, who knew no sin, became for a moment in time the worst of all sinners. There never lived a man more blamed who lived more blamelessly.

"He was oppressed, and he was afflicted" (Isaiah 53:7).

Whatever else, Jesus was the freest man who ever lived. His choices never once infringed His agency. Yet He surrendered that liberty and became a prisoner for us. No man more free was ever more oppressed than He.

"[H]e opened not his mouth" (Isaiah 53:7).

He never defended Himself. Never through all of history could so much have been spoken in a condemned man's defense when so little was.

"[H]e was cut off," Isaiah said, "out of the land of the living" (Isaiah 53:8).

Has there ever lived a man through all the ages with a greater power to live, and live nobly, who died more painfully and shamefully than Jesus did?

"[H]e made his grave with the wicked" (Isaiah 53:9).

Consider that! The almighty king of heaven and earth came to earth and was sold as a slave, died as a criminal, and buried as the most abject of commoners—consider the cruelty of that!

"[I]t pleased the LORD to bruise Him" (Isaiah 53:10).

Just think about that! God, who is love and the kindest of all, gave His most beloved and favored Son the cruelest burden any man ever bore. That is an irony.

Just as Jesus was not what they expected in the Savior, so too are we sometimes shocked when following Him leads us where we least expect, to pain we don't deserve, and through disappointments we can scarcely bear.

It would be well for you, beloved Saint, to sear this sentence into your soul and live by it: *I believe in Christ, so come what may.*

I testify as you love the Lord, it probably will.

And remember this: He who descended below all things rose above all things—as will you!

The Parable of the Map

There was once a man trapped in misery and terrible poverty, though he did not know the full extent of it. One day a carrier came to his door with a letter and a package. He opened the letter. It was from a friend and distant relative from so long ago he barely remembered him. The letter told him that his friend had come into a vast fortune and wanted to share it with him. It was huge—millions! For his part, the man was only to come and claim his inheritance. Visions of what he would spend such a fortune on filled his mind. Oh, the things he would buy and the comfort he would purchase.

But the letter did not say where He was to go or how to get there. "All you need to know," the letter said cryptically, "is found in the book." With that, the messenger handed him the package.

The man tore open the package and found a very ordinary-looking book, dog-eared from heavy use. Eager for his treasure, the man opened the book and began to read. But what was this? The language was difficult and made no sense. But the lure of the treasure enticed him, and he kept reading. After some time, he realized the book was a collection of stories and reflections written by those who had before made the same journey he was now invited to undertake.

"I don't understand," he questioned. "They all traveled from different places than me. How can they help me?"

Soon, familiarity made the stories easier to understand. He began to enjoy the book. Then, one day it happened. One man's story seemed to come to life for him. His heart burned with excitement as he poured over the man's adventure. He was intensely drawn to the man's account of receiving the treasure. It became so real. And with that, he packed his meager belongings and set out, filled with the fire the story had kindled.

It was a journey of many years that took him through many lands, across various continents, and into different cultures of people. At times, his interest waned, and the book became boring. He had read all the stories before. At those times he felt lost but did not know why. But something always drew him back to the book.

Good things happened when he looked to the book, but it frustrated him that they were so infrequent and accidental. And so he went for many years, until one day he found himself stranded in a desolate and dark wilderness. The climate was cold and bleak, the people hostile and threatening. He was hopelessly lost and more miserable than before he had begun the journey. He became weakened and discouraged. For the first time since leaving his home, he began to wonder if his friend had lied to him, and he was going to die out here.

On one particularly difficult night, he lay down under the stars and pulled out his book. As he read, he felt that familiar comfort and reassurance come back to him. Suddenly, he sat up abruptly and looked around at his surroundings. With joy he realized that the man whose story he was reading was describing the exact place where he was stranded. It thrilled him as he picked out each of the landmarks the man described. Voraciously, he devoured the rest of the story, examining with careful detail every word and nuance. Sure enough, the former traveler revealed the way out.

Since leaving his home, he had wandered, knowing at times he was close to where he was supposed to be, but never quite sure. Now he had his bearings and knew exactly where he was and in which direction to travel. Straight as a course can be set, he journeyed on, gaining much ground. Upon arrival at his next destination, he did it again, tearing into the book, looking for clues to see if someone had already been here as well. His search was rewarded immediately.

Presently, the realization settled on him that he had been using the book wrong all these years. This was not a book intended to entertain or just make him feel good. It was indeed a map and should be used as such. With new eyes, he began to study the book. Confidence filled him such that no matter where he went, a previous traveler had been there and would point the way. No longer was the book a duty. It became a passion, and he lived by its every word. As he did so, he journeyed in an undeviating course, the vision of the treasure seeming to loom larger in his mind. He could see little else.

Finally, he arrived. The face of his friend was as familiar as if they had always been together. His inheritance was given to him. He turned to go, and his friend called after him. "Now that you are wealthy, what will you buy?"

"As I journeyed," the traveler said, "I passed through many lands and met many people. They were very poor and miserable." The man stopped speaking, as tears filled his eyes. "I'm going back to them now... to share."

Nebuchadnezzar's Humbling

It is a true principle that if we start right it is easy to go right, but if we start wrong we go wrong, and it's hard to get right (Joseph Smith, *History of the Church*, 6:303).

Therefore, trying to obtain spirituality without first obtaining humility is like trying to grow potatoes on concrete. For God resists the proud and gives grace to the humble (see James 4:6). Humility comes from the root *humus*, which means "earth." So, to humble yourself is not only to bring your heart down to the ground, but also to prepare the ground of your heart. And God will have a humble people—just ask Nebuchadnezzar.

King Nebuchadnezzar of Babylon was a powerful man (see Daniel 4). One day, he had a dream and saw a great tree that towered in magnificence so high that it touched heaven and could be seen from anywhere. All living things were nurtured by it. Then came a voice commanding that the tree be cut down to the ground.

Neb was troubled and asked Daniel what it meant. Daniel revealed that the tree was Neb himself. He was to be the one leveled to the earth to become as a beast.

"Break off thy sins," Daniel pleaded, and "show mercy unto the poor. If it may be a lengthening of thy tranquility" (Daniel 4:27).

But Neb didn't take the warning seriously. "Is not this great Babylon that I have built for the house of the kingdom by the might of my power, and for the honor of my majesty?" he boasted (Daniel 4:30). In other words, "Man, I'm good."

Before he even finished the sentence, a voice fell from heaven. "The kingdom is departed from thee . . . until thou know the most

High ruleth" (Daniel 4:31–32). Within the hour, Neb lost his reason and became as a dumb ox, eating grass and living in the fields. For seven years the dew wet his body. His hair went uncut and his fingernails unclipped. The most exalted man in the world was abased in a moment.

One day, Nebuchadnezzar looked up to heaven. His reason returned, and he was restored to his kingdom, becoming greater than before.

Humbled, he made a proclamation to the world: "I . . . praise and extol and honor the King of heaven . . . and those that walk in pride He is able to abase" (Daniel 4:37).

If you would be close to God, cut down the tree of your ego before He does. Remember, every knee will bow because every towering ego will be toppled.

Old Mustard

My old pickup is a 1972 Chevrolet two-wheel drive, otherwise affectionately known as "Old Mustard." I've had it for a long time. Many cars have come and gone through the Rawson household through the years, but Old Mustard has outlived them all. The others were fancier, they were more comfortable, they had more features—but they're gone now, and he isn't.

Winter to summer, he sits outside, not in the garage, and yet he is the one who has always started, always been there in a pinch. When the real work needs to be done, we always turn to Old Mustard, and he always gets it done.

Battle-scarred? He is the ugliest truck in the country! There is nothing even remotely handsome about him! We had a contest one time among my students to see who could get the exact count on how many colors he sports. We lost count at twenty-three. But since then, he has been wrecked twice and rebuilt, and the shades of rust and primer have deepened and hued over time. He is homely, but he's a tough old warrior.

He has taught each of my children to drive. He's been an excellent teacher—dents included. Somehow, he has endured gracefully the dents, the grinding gears, the folded bumpers, and the leveled telephone poles. He has taken us faithfully to beautiful, scenic places; pulled our camp trailers; and served us as no other.

He's low-maintenance—he always has been! Oh, sure—we've had to do some repairs once in a while along the way, but nothing compared to these other pieces of plastic that I drive. The fact is, in some respects, this old truck is better now than he was when he was built!

Now, I don't know if you should love a piece of machinery, but we love him! Each of my children wants him. They argue over who gets him when I'm dead. I finally settled the argument by telling them that when I go, I want to be buried in him as my casket.

Now, he's plain; he's ordinary. He will never be anything but a work truck. There's nothing aspiring or pretentious about him. He is exactly what you see! But what you will never see is how faithful to the work he has been for more years than any of my children have been alive. A Hummer he is not. A Ram he will never be. No one will ever whistle in admiration when he goes by. But if there's a heaven for old trucks, he surely belongs there.

I've had numerous offers to buy him. We've turned them all down. It would take more money than I can afford to replace him. Besides, I know this sounds kind of over-the-top, but how do you replace a trusted and true friend?

I hope you know that this story is a parable. Yes, I'm talking about my old truck, but I'm really talking about us as servants of the Lord. You might not be the best looking, the most talented, with the most to give. You might be downright homely, with low talent, just like Old Mustard. It isn't how you look that matters; it's what you give.

As Old Mustard has given for my family, so I hope we will all give for the Lord and His family the tranquil, steady dedication of service—for a lifetime.

So let's get it in gear, and get to work!

Cell Phones and Prayer

Recently, while traveling through western Montana, I heard a beep and reached for my cell phone. The battery was fading fast. I hooked it up to DC power, but it still would not work. For the first time in a long time, and for the rest of a somewhat long trip, I was out of touch. I could not call a soul, and they could not reach me. It was an odd feeling that I have not experienced in quite some time. I felt strangely alone.

The first touches of a feeling of melancholy set in. I began to imagine all manner of crises that might be occurring among those I love. What if one of them was injured? What if they really needed me and I was not there? What if I got back home and my world had become chaos in my absence?

Then another thought struck me. What if no one missed me at all? Melancholy came over me then like a wet, cold blanket. It's strange how cell phones have become so connected to our hearts. Through them, we are empowered to hold our loved ones close and be there no matter where we are. Recently, when my son was in the Caribbean, he gave me a vocal and picture tour of the luxury liner he was on while I sat in envy in the January cold of Idaho.

These days it seems that as many people as have ears have cell phones. The money, time, and energy being expended just to stay in touch are staggering. I've even seen people talking on their phones on top of the Grand Teton.

What manner of people would we be if we were equally concerned about staying close to God as we are with each other? If we worried as much about being out of touch with Him as much as we worry about missing a call from a friend, perhaps He would be our friend as well as our Father. Richard L. Evans said, "He who ceases to pray loses a great friend." By and through prayer, we can have a sweet and beautiful relationship with our Father in Heaven. As we draw near to Him, He will draw near unto us.

However, when we stop praying with real intent or stop praying altogether, the dearness of that friendship fades as surely as falling out of touch with your high school friends.

Unlike your cell phone, the minutes of your prayer plan truly are unlimited—you really can call anytime and as often as you choose. In fact, you are commanded to call daily, even always. However, it is not free and not to be trifled with. If we ask Him for help, He expects us to listen. Fair-weather friends who call only in moments of crisis or convenience and just because they want something are just as obnoxious to heaven above as they are to us as mortals below. Moreover, we do not pray just to chat. Granted, we are to come to Him as family and speak openly and honestly, but prayer is our vital connection to the power of a world greater than this one, a world we all want. Prayer brings us into the circle of His arms, and we know His love.

To return to my story, I got back home late that day and had my phone repaired. I turned it on, and it rang immediately. I had been missed. Several people had been trying to reach me, and there had indeed been a minor crisis. I was needed.

I am grateful for the technology that keeps me in touch with those I love, but I am more grateful that I know how to pray and that God is our Father and friend. Family and friends could do fine without us, but we should never do without Him. Greater than a cell phone, prayer is the most powerful communication known to man.

The Least of These

Do you remember when Jesus said, "he shall set the sheep on his right hand, but the goats on the left" (Matthew 25:33)?

I want to be one of those sheep on His right hand. What is it that these faithful sons and daughters have done that have so won the Savior's gratitude and favor that He puts them on His right hand? What is it that we can do to be the most prepared for the Second Coming of Christ?

Here's the answer: "For I was an hungred and ye gave me meat: I was thirsty, and ye gave me drink: I was a stranger, and ye took me in: Naked, and ye clothed me: I was sick, and ye visited me: I was in prison, and ye came unto me" (Matthew 25:35–36).

The faithful will hear all these things, and they will wonder, "Well, when did we do these things for you, Lord?" And He will answer, "Verily I say unto you, Inasmuch as ye have done it unto one of the least of these my brethren, ye have done it unto me" (Matthew 25:40).

In other words, we do it with simple things—kindly acts of ministering, such as giving away our time, our talents, our means, and our love to the people around us each day. Those deemed the least in society will bring us to inherit the greatest of all God's gifts.

Some time ago, I was traveling alone to Salt Lake City when I was struck with a familiar, stabbing pain in my back. It was a kidney stone. I'd had one before, and I knew I was in trouble. The pain was terrible, and I was almost twenty-five miles from the nearest hospital. I turned around and started back. I made it, but barely.

While in the emergency room, they ran some tests, and it was confirmed that indeed I did have a kidney stone. But then the doctor surprised me by saying, "You also have pneumonia!"

The next few days are a blur. I cannot remember in more than thirty years being that sick for that long. I sank lower and lower until I could not get up.

As I lay there sick and weak from fever, I felt something touch my forehead. I opened my tear-filled eyes, and I saw our seven-year-old son Adam standing over me with his hand on my forehead and a very serious expression on his little face. He was checking my temperature.

I know he had no idea what he was doing. But because his mother had done this for him when he was sick, he knew that this was something you did for sick people. As my illness progressed and deepened, he came and checked my temperature often. When I needed medications, he fetched them. And then when all else failed to make me well, he came in filled with concern, laid down beside me, wrapped his arms around me, and said, "I love you, Dad."

I laid there and wept! I will never forget his kindness. It didn't heal my body, but it lifted my spirits. And to me at the time, that mattered the most!

You know, my friends, I wonder sometimes if the Lord cares as much about what we say in church as what we do at home and in the world.

Pain

In Gethsemane, the Lord Jesus suffered pain of body and spirit in totality. It caused Him to sweat blood and shrink, but He saw it through. Then Judas, a friend, betrayed Him with a kiss.

Peter grabbed his sword and rushed to defend the Savior. But the Savior stopped him, saying, "Thinkest thou that I cannot now pray to my Father, and he shall presently give me more than twelve legions of angels?" (Matthew 26:53).

Jesus knew the suffering ahead of Him, and yet not only did He go willingly to the scourging and the cross, He wouldn't allow anyone to take it from Him. Roman soldiers led Jesus up Golgotha's hill to crucify Him. Crucifixion was torture! It was agony!

Before they nailed Him to the cross, they offered Him a drink of vinegar mingled with gall, and when He had tasted the vinegar, He wouldn't drink. Gall was a drug that was intended to deaden the pain. So why did the Savior refuse it? Because He wanted the pain. He had to have it, all of it—all of ours for all of us.

Jesus was crucified for the sins of the world. The cross was part of His Atonement by which He paid for our sins and redeemed us. His suffering was essential to an infinite Atonement.

There is pain of the body, and there is pain of the spirit. It is our nature as mortals that when we hurt, we want it to go away. The health-care industry is a testament to the price we are willing to pay for remedies to our pain. When I hurt, personally, all I can think of is ending the pain—now!

Pain can be healed, avoided, or ignored. Jesus did none of these. His incomprehensible pain had purpose, and He invited it. And as a perfect man, He felt everything perfectly; nothing diminished His anguish. Moreover, the Father gave Jesus a greater measure of pain for His mortal sojourn than any other person has ever borne. And Jesus bore it meekly.

Isaiah used the word *bear* deliberately when he said, "Surely he hath borne our griefs and carried our sorrows. . . . By his knowledge shall my righteous servant justify many; for he shall bear their iniquities . . . he bare the sin of many" (Isaiah 53: 4, 11, 12).

Oh, it is wonderful what He bore! I stand all amazed that He stood it. By His pain I live; by my own pain I learn.

Praise be to God for pain. And for you who are in pain, patience—it will pass.

The President

On May 30, 1787, a small group of men in Philadelphia changed the world. They were the delegates to the Constitutional Convention. Among other things, they created an officer of government unlike any ever before, one destined to become the most powerful political figure in our modern world — the President of the United States.

"There must be one, and not three," they said. The office would require energy, action, and decisiveness. With only one, we would always know who's responsible, and once a year he was expected to report to the people.

They were going to call him "His Excellency." But that wouldn't do. The President of the United States is a man of the people, a leader among equals.

Four years he would serve, and then he would be returned to his people, and that was the design. The Framers felt if he merited their esteem, they could have him again as president. The only limit on his term was to be the wisdom of the people who elected him.

It was considered that he not even receive a salary, but sometimes the best of men are not wealthy men. He was to serve for love and honor, not for love of money.

The Framers put him under the most sacred oath to preserve, protect, and defend the Constitution. To preserve that document, they felt, was to save us as a nation.

Never — never was the president to start a war! He could defend us in case of attack, but he could not start a war. If the blood and money of the people were to be expended in war, the people must declare it. But once it was declared, he was the Commander-in-Chief.

No law was ever to be imposed on us without his approval — no treaty that he did not negotiate. He was to be our voice to the nation, the champion of our rights and liberties, and the guardian — the guardian of all his people.

He alone was to be the nation's voice of mercy and reason through the pardon power. All the chief officers who execute the law and judge it were to be his appointees — his nominees. He was to be the one man in government above the pettiness of partisan politics. He was not to be a man of the party, but a man for us all.

So critical was his leadership, and so vital his virtue, that the Framers did not trust the common people to find him and elect him. So they devised a system whereby the wisest among us would select the wisest to be him.

He had to be a native son, a fully imbued American, filled with wisdom, maturity, goodness, and integrity. He was to be our voice, our protector, and the great man of the people.

He would be, and still is, only as powerful as "we the people." Similarly, he is only as good as we are. And the nation would be ever after as safe and free as he was good, honest, and wise.

Few men living can affect more people in a deeper way for a longer time than the President of the United States. Therefore, all things considered, God help us to be wise as we cast our votes!

If I Lose My Way

If the Lord delights in the song of the heart, then He must equally delight in the heart that writes the song. Well, this is the story of an inspired song.

A few years ago, a friend of mine, Fay, was a sad and lonely college student, lost in the vastness of a huge university. Fay is also a songwriter.

One day a song that she had previously written came back to her mind and seemed to press itself upon her. There was a lyric that she felt she just had to write into that song, even though it would alter the theme.

The lyric said, "If I lose my way, will you come find me? If I forget who I am, will you remind me?"

Well, she wrote it. But then when she tried to make the rest of the song fit the new theme, it wouldn't fit. Inspiration just wouldn't come. She worked and she pondered; finally, she asked the Lord to help her.

And then, two days later, on a Sunday morning at 6 a.m., she was awakened by a commotion outside her window. Groggy with sleep, she sat up in bed and looked down from her cramped second-story attic apartment and saw a police officer, a police car, and a very old man. The old man was standing in the brisk morning air wearing nothing but his undergarments.

"What are you doing!" the officer asked in a rough voice.

The old man, looking like a lost little boy, responded with a helpless shrug of his shoulders, but he said nothing.

"What's your name?" the officer asked in a voice a little less rough.

Again, a blank shrug of the shoulders was the only response.

"Where do you live?" This time the voice was gentle and entreating.

But another shrug was the only reply.

And then it came: Understanding washed over Fay like the light of dawn, and her eyes filled with burning tears. Here was this sweet old man who had probably lived a long and a full life of service, and now he was lost, he was alone, and he was literally out in the cold. Where was his family? Were they looking for him even at that moment? Was anyone looking for him?

Humbled to the depths and feeling almost like an intruder, Fay watched quietly as the officer helped the old man into his car and drove him away. She was suddenly filled with the feeling that she just wanted to go down and help him; she just wanted to rescue him—do something for him! The poor man!

She sank back into her bed, and her tears changed to sobs. But now they weren't just for the old man; they were for her. She was just like him. She knew her name, of course. She knew her address. But she was lost! She was empty and disconnected from her Heavenly Father.

Overcome by it all, she lie there in bed and just let the tears roll, and the image of the old man burned itself into her brain. She went to church and cried all through the meetings, unable to forget him.

Somewhere in the coming hours and days, it came to her. This was it. This was the answer to her prayers. The Lord wanted Fay to finish that song, and now she could. Over the next few days, line upon line, the song came to be. And through the course of writing that song, inspired by the old man, Fay too found her way home.

She wrote in the song, "And if I lose my way, He will come find me. If I forget who I am, He will remind me. It's a long, long road, and I don't have to make it on my own."

As a servant of the Lord, I testify that we do not have to traverse the path of life alone. There is an iron rod nearby. The mists of darkness will come, but they do not need to disorient us. Remember, and remember always, the light of the world is just up ahead.

From the experience of Fay Belnap

A Father's Prayer

I don't believe there is a day that goes by but what I am reminded, as a father, of the great, awesome, and inescapable responsibility it is to be a father. I am keenly aware that I will be held strictly accountable for my actions in relation to my family. Therefore, it is my constant prayer that my children will cherish what I cherish and serve as I have tried to serve. I don't believe that I'm alone as a father in such sentiments. Years ago, these lines were penned by General Douglas MacArthur. They are classic, and where he refers to son, I would add daughter as well. He said:

"Build me a son, O Lord, who will be strong enough to know when he is weak, and brave enough to face himself when he is afraid; one who will be proud of unbending in honest defeat, and humble and gentle in victory.

"Build me a son, whose wishbone will not be where his backbone should be, a son who will know Thee — and that to know himself is the foundation stone of knowledge.

"Lead him, I pray, not in the path of ease and comfort, but under the stress and spur of difficulties and challenge. Here let him learn to stand up in the storm, here let him learn compassion for those who fail.

"Build me a son whose heart will be clear, whose goal will be high; a son who will master himself before he seeks to master other men; one who will learn to laugh, yet never forget how to weep; one who will reach into the future, yet never forget the past.

"After all these things are his, add, I pray, enough of a sense of humor, so that he may not always be serious, yet never take himself too seriously. Give him humility, so that he may always remember the simplicity of true greatness, the open mind of true wisdom, the meekness of true strength.

"Then, I, his father, will dare to whisper, 'I have not lived in vain.'"

Now, to those fathers whose lives are worn out in service to and yearning for their families each day, as my noble father did, I salute you and ask you to remember one thing: "One cannot raise heaven's child without heaven's help."

HE WAS GONE

We speak sometimes of those who waste and wear out their lives for the Lord's sake. Let me tell you of one man whom history has all but forgotten.

Lorenzo Dow Barnes was born in 1812 in Tolland, Massachusetts, the son of Phineas, a New England farmer. He was named for Lorenzo Dow, the great eighteenth-century revivalist. In 1815, his family moved to Ohio, where in 1833, he was taught the gospel and baptized. Immediately after his baptism he went out as a missionary. When the Lord called for volunteers to march with Zion's Camp to redeem Zion in 1834, Lorenzo volunteered. Upon his return, Lorenzo was among the first seventies called in this dispensation.

After his call, he set out again as a missionary. It is said that the twenty-three-year-old missionary had limited education and a speech impediment; he stuttered, which caused enemies of the Church to single him out for attack. Evidently, Lorenzo did not back down and engaged in numerous debates with opposing clergymen. Not only did those debates ultimately yield baptisms, but Lorenzo overcame his weakness and became a powerful orator.

In 1838, he was ordained a high priest and was called to be a missionary in the eastern and southern United States, where he traveled without purse or scrip and established several branches of the Church.

In 1841, Elder Barnes led a company of Saints to Nauvoo, where he courted and married Susan Conrad. Shortly after his marriage, he was called to serve as a missionary in England. While serving as president of the Bradford Conference, Elder Lorenzo Barnes passed away. He was thirty years old. It was said of him that was "possessed of most untiring perseverance, industry, and application and wore out his life by constant preaching and exposure."

After his death, the local Saints, led by Elder Wilford Woodruff, took up a collection and erected a stone memorial over his grave in Idle, Yorkshire. It reads:

"In memory of Lorenzo D. Barnes, who died on the 20th of December 1842, age 30 years. He was a native of the United States, an Elder in the Church of Jesus Christ of Latter-day Saints, a member of the High Priests Quorum and also of Zion's Camp in the year 1834, and the first gospel messenger from Nauvoo who has found a grave in a foreign land."

Lorenzo Barnes was the first missionary of The Church of Jesus Christ of Latter-day Saints to give his life on foreign soil. He would not be the last. He left behind a wife, no children, and an undeniable legacy.

When the Prophet Joseph Smith learned of Lorenzo's death, he lamented:

> When I heard of the death of our beloved bro Barns it would not have affected me so much if I had the opportunity of burying him in the land of Zion. I believe, those who have buried their friends here, their condition is enviable. Look at Joseph in Egypt how he required his friends to bury him in the tomb of his fathers.

Later, money was donated, and the remains of Elder Barnes were brought to Utah and re-interred in the Salt Lake City Cemetery—among his friends and family.

Sources: https://familypedia.wikia.org/wiki/Lorenzo_Dow_Barnes_(1812-1842) https://www.familysearch.org/tree/person/memories/KWVW-YF2

Tumbleweeds

Some time ago on a blustery day, my family and I were traveling across the state. The first 130 miles of the trip had been a continuous rainstorm, but as we continued east, we outran the storm and reached its leading edge. There we encountered high winds, broadsiding the freeway. These were the kinds of winds that make driving a minivan in the proper lane a concentrated effort.

At one point, something momentarily distracted me. I glanced away for only a moment. When I looked back, a huge tumbleweed came out of nowhere and landed on the highway. There was no way I could miss it. There are probably still pieces of that thing stuck in the grill of my van.

Looking down the highway, I observed nearly a dozen tumbleweeds rolling and bouncing across the freeway. It looked like the high-desert version of a coastal hurricane.

Looking off to my right, it appeared as though the desert floor was alive. Tumbleweeds were rolling and bouncing everywhere amid blowing clouds of choking dust. Some sailed over the fence and across the Interstate, but most became lodged in the fence.

I thought back to my boyhood days on the ranch and the problems tumbleweeds caused. They were useless as feed for the stock and often ruined good grazing land. Additionally, after they ripened and dried out, strong winds broke them loose from their roots and carried them off. Every year huge piles of tumbleweeds clogged our fences and ditches, requiring the fences to be cleaned and the ditches to be burned.

There is a lesson in tumbleweeds.

It seems we live in a tumbleweed world. There are individuals and societies letting go of those principles and values that root them in place and ensure their safety. Too many let go of their gospel roots and are blown about with every wind of fad, fashion, and opinion. Back and forth they go until they are no more.

The thrill of rolling morally "free" may be a fun frolic, but it is always a short-lived tragedy. If such people do not return to God, they will, like the tumbleweeds, find themselves piled up like the rest of the crowd waiting for the fire—which will surely come.

God bids us to "stand in holy places." If you are already in place, hold fast, and sink those roots even deeper. If you are not anchored in place, look down the road. Are you going where you know you should? Come unto Christ and become rooted and grounded in Him. Then you will learn what it means to have your own roots and branches in the day that He comes. As it grows late in the season and everything around us ripens, what would you be—a drifting tumbleweed or a fruitful tree?

The Hearts of the Children

Memorial Day was established to cause us to remember and honor those who have gone before us.

After the Civil War, there were those who wanted to remember and honor fallen Union soldiers. Eventually, that sentiment expanded to include all those who had died in any war. Today, Memorial Day is a national holiday where we remember all those that we have loved and lost.

Personally, when I visit family graves, my memory is renewed with love for them, even those I didn't know. And for those I did know, life's experiences with them return. Their hallowed graves touch this child's heart and turn it to his father's each time I go.

In the spirit of Memorial Day, I'd like to share something that you may not have considered before.

We are the children of the prophets, and I promise you it matters a great deal to our ancient fathers that we do not forget them and their legacy.

There were many, but I'll mention just a few. Some seven hundred years before Christ, the great prophet Isaiah was killed for his testimony of the Messiah. He died a martyr—a witness. Then Peter, the Savior's chief Apostle, was crucified upside down, also for being a witness of Christ. James was run through with a sword. Paul was beheaded. Nearly all of the Savior's Apostles died violent deaths for their witness of Christ. They gave their lives, effectively sealing, making permanent, their testimonies for all time (see Hebrews 9:16–17).

The single greatest expression of testimony is for the witness to voluntarily give his life for it.

These were not the last martyrs.

On June 27, 1844, an enraged mob stormed a small jail in Carthage, Illinois. When their fury was through, two innocent men lay dead—two men who bore the same witness as Peter and James and who died for the same reasons. Their innocent blood is now an ambassador.

In light of what I've said, think about the Savior's words through Malachi: "Behold I will send you Elijah the prophet before the coming of the great and dreadful day of the Lord; and he shall turn the hearts of the fathers to the children and the hearts of the children to their fathers, lest I come and smite the earth with a curse" (Malachi 4:5–6).

Memorial Day originated to honor those slain for freedom. Well, what of those slain for the word of the Lord? I can't go to the graves of the ancient ones, but I can go to their testimonies. The holy scriptures cost the lives of the best men of their times. Therefore, it behooves us as grateful children that we turn our hearts to our prophet fathers with a greater reverence for the written memorial they left us. And when we do, we will be led to Him who will bring life again to all men.

The Nobleman's Son

If you find yourself right now in need of God, but aren't getting the answers you want, I'd like to share a story.

One day, Jesus came into the little town of Cana of Galilee, where He was met by a nobleman. It seems that this man's son was dying. He desperately begged Jesus to come down and heal his son. The son was twenty miles away in Capernaum. What the father wanted was for Jesus, right then and there, to travel to Capernaum and lay His hands on the boy and heal him.

What happened next in the story is intriguing. Instead of commending the man for his faith in coming in the first place, Jesus chides him, saying, "Except ye see signs and wonders, ye will not believe" (John 4:48).

The man was not offended, but rather he persisted, saying, "Sir, come down ere my child die" (John 4:49).

Why did Jesus rebuke him? It's obvious he had faith. But maybe Jesus rebuked him because this man is like so many of us. He came to Jesus for help, telling Jesus where, when, and how that help was to be delivered. In his mind, unless Jesus was physically there in Capernaum, the boy couldn't be healed. But Jesus is so much more than this man ever imagined. He is Lord of the universe! He has all power, all knowledge; with Him indeed all things are possible. It seems audacious to put God in a box!

Well, Jesus, stretching the man's faith, said, "Go thy way; thy son liveth" (John 4:50).

The man believed the Lord's healing word, and he set out for home. On the way, he was met by his servants, who announced that his son was indeed on the mend. When he asked them when the boy began to heal, he was informed that it was the seventh hour, the exact same moment that Jesus had spoken.

He went for a miracle of healing and returned converted to the gospel—he and all his household. He, like so many of us, can get far more than we set out for if we'll just remember—there are no limits to God! He can do anything for us He wants to if we will let Him. His ways are not our ways. They're better!

You can see that to surrender your stubborn will to God in faith is to set both of you free. Oh, may it be.

Kassie's Soap

If you think there's nothing special about you—that you are common, ordinary, garden variety, and vanilla—I have something to say about your uniqueness.

I was teaching a college institute class. It was a new semester, and I asked the class members to share their name and something unique about them as a way of getting familiar with each other. It's a way of just learning names and trying to remember them. Well, we went around the room and we listened to each student. Most of the comments about what they thought was unique about them were very entertaining.

I then came to one young mother. She announced that she had a condition called pica. What in the world is pica? I was thinking of some little rodent up in the mountains. She then explained that pica is a condition that causes her when pregnant to crave nonedible things—to eat them. In her case, she craves soap. That's right—soap! She wants to eat soap. And not just any soap will do; she craves Irish Spring! Well, by this time, the class was laughing uncontrollably! And then to top it off, Kassie announced that she was expecting, and that this was a current situation!

I guess I was having a hard time believing this, because I hadn't heard of it. "You really do eat the soap?" I asked.

She said, "No, I just rub the soap on the box and then chew on the box."

"How does your husband feel about all this?" I asked.

"He was a little traumatized by it during the first pregnancy, but then he decided to go with it. Now he just rubs the soap all over his face."

Well, the class just lost it! I laughed so hard tears came to my eyes. That is one genius of a husband.

I have been unable to forget that story. It keeps coming back to me, and every time I think about it, I start laughing again. So, I hope that you won't mind if I share a principle, something I learned that came to me from Kassie's story.

We are children of God. I mean that. We are children of God; we're not biological accidents, and we're not mutant monkeys. Each of us is indeed unique in the full and complete sense of that word. There are things about us found nowhere else in the human family. And the closer we get to the God who made us, the more He brings out our individuality.

Wickedness is sameness; righteousness is the only true individuality. Not only has God the Father blessed each of us to be delightfully different, but—like Kassie's enterprising husband—God knows full well how to take advantage of our uniqueness for His blessing and for ours.

To paraphrase Paul, I may not be the head, but I can be the big toe of the body of Christ's Church, and just let that body try to do without me. It can't.

So, my dear friends, go find your own soap, and make the most out of it.

SAUL

In my lifetime, I have met some wonderfully talented people with great abilities in everything from the fine arts to the industrial arts. All these people have made their contribution in one way or another to the human race. But there is one, it recently occurred to me, who has perfected the talent of humanity; He has perfected people. It is the Lord Jesus Christ. He is "mighty to save and cleanse us." There is no one who loves us more, who has a greater desire to help us, and more power to do so than He.

Who would have thought in 34 A.D. that Saul of Tarsas would become a Christian? If you read the story, if ever there was a man who was anti-Christ, and an unlikely Christian, it was Saul.

When the devout Christian Stephen was stoned by the Jews for his testimony of Jesus, it was Saul who stood by as a witness and consented to the murder.

It was Saul who made such havoc of the Church in Jerusalem that the Christians in that city were scattered from the city for their own safety.

It was Saul who took men and women of Christ and put them in prison for their faith.

It was Saul who was so active and so zealous in his persecution of the Saints that he was known and feared far beyond the confines of the city of Jerusalem.

It was Saul who vehemently continued to breathe out threatenings and slaughter against the disciples of the Lord.

Surely, if ever there was a man who was an unlikely candidate for Christianity, it had to have been Saul.

That is until one day on the road to Damascus on a mission to further persecute the Christians, a brilliant and blinding light shone round about him, causing him to fall to the earth. He heard a voice say to him, "Saul, Saul, why persecutest thou me?" (Acts 9:4).

Saul answered, "Who art thou, Lord?" (Acts 9:5).

"I am Jesus whom thou persecutest" (Acts 9:5).

Trembling and astonished, Saul asked, "what wilt thou have me to do, [Lord?]" (Acts 9:6).

That question and the Lord's answer to it changed Saul forever. He changed by the grace of Christ from Saul, the persecutor of Christ, to Paul, the Apostle of Christ. It's interesting to me that he who consented to the death of the Christian martyr Stephen himself eventually died a Christian martyr.

What about you and me? May I humbly ask, if we call Jesus Lord and Savior, do we have faith in His power to save us, and the ones we love?

Based on Acts 9 and Acts 26.

Lincoln's Proposal

While we tend to want unending happy hearts and contented days, our Father in Heaven wants something greater for us, and the pathway to that is a broken heart and a contrite spirit.

The story is told of Abraham Lincoln and his courtship of Mary Owens. Abe had met Mary several years before through an association with a friend. Well, following a tragedy in his life, Lincoln's friend suggested that Abe and Mary would make a fine couple; the friend was willing to travel to Kentucky and bring Mary back. Abe was much in favor of the idea. However, when Mary Owens arrived, she was far different from what Abe remembered, having gained considerable weight.

Try as he might, Lincoln could not persuade himself to fall in love with Mary Owens. He tried to convince himself that the brilliancy of her mind eclipsed her size, which it evidently did, but the desired flame of love would still not kindle.

He was a man in trouble! He had committed, sight unseen, to marry her. He procrastinated the proposal until finally in a letter he asked for her hand. I suspect no woman has ever received a proposal worded quite like this one. This is what he wrote:

> This thing of living in Springfield is rather a dull business after all. I'm afraid you would not be satisfied. There's a great deal of flourishing about in carriages here, which it would be your doom to see without sharing in it. You would have to be poor without the means of hiding your poverty. Do you believe you could bare that patiently?
>
> What I have said I will most positively abide by—provided you wish it. My opinion is that you had better not do it. You have

not been accustomed to hardship, and it may be more severe than you now image.

Yours, Lincoln

Mary Owens turned him down. Lincoln was surprised by the rejection and a little broken-hearted, probably more at the blow to his ego than the infatuation of his heart. He resolved "never again to think of marrying," and for this reason, "I can never be satisfied with anyone who would be block-head[ed] enough to have me."

Well, fortunately for Lincoln and history, he met Mary Todd shortly after, and they were married. She healed his heart and gave him to history as the great emancipator.

All men set their hearts on something or someone, and because some of us set our hearts on the things of this fallen natural world, we're called natural men. And it is for that reason that all men must experience a broken heart and a contrite spirit. Hearts set on natural things must first be broken to then be bound on heavenly things.

My friends, our greatness here and in the hereafter will be directly connected to our willingness to let God have His way with our hearts right now.

Road Trip

Recently, I experienced what could only be called a sensory adventure. I began that day standing on the lush green banks of the North Platte River near Glenrock, Wyoming—the old Pioneer Trail. The river ran slowly and was rife with birds and vegetation. It was beautiful!

Then I headed west, crossing Wyoming's high desert at nearly six thousand feet in elevation. It was hot and unbelievably dry! The vegetation out there was sparse, low-growing sage and bunch grass. It was as opposite from the North Platte as anything you can imagine, but the contrast was the beauty!

It was in a place such as this that Moses and Abraham found their God.

As I rolled on west, I climbed three thousand feet up into the mountains. I rolled down my window and caught the rich, wonderful aroma of pine and fir. I pulled over close to the summit of Togwotee Pass and walked about two hundred feet off the road into the trees. I was swallowed by the forest, and from then on all I heard were the sounds of nature: scolding squirrels, singing birds, creaking trees. I stood atop a high bluff, and I could hear the unique sound of the descending mountain stream below me. I love music, but there are few compositions that can compare with that.

I looked down, and there at my feet noticed the last drops of a recent rain trapped in a trough of lupine leaves. I knelt down. The rich, alpine soil was as soft and fluffed as a pillow. I offered a quick and quiet prayer. As I did so, the sun came out and felt like an oven-warmed blanket on my back. With my eyes closed, I became conscious then of a gentle breeze sweeping up the mountain. It was like a cooling caress.

I moved on. Down the mountains I went into Jackson Hole. As I journeyed south through the valley, the Tetons loomed off to my right. I can see why the early explorers called them the "pilot knobs."

Any traveler within eyeshot can get his bearings if he'll just look up. Maybe that's why God created such things—so we would look up once in a while, think higher, and be inspired by something besides the worldly and mundane. The Tetons? You had to see it! They were shrouded like ancient Sinai in dark storm clouds, adding all the more to their mystery and majesty. I couldn't get enough.

Then it was on through the Snake River Canyon and along the South Fork, where the river rafters and fisherman like to play. It is this river where sunlight so often sparkles off that water to make one think it is a river of diamonds.

And then, from the palisades above Palisades Reservoir, I stared down with appreciation noting how the water, usually blue, reflected now the iron gray of the thunderstorm above it.

By then it was late in the day, and I was almost home. Coming along Interstate 15, my window down, all of a sudden I caught the sweet, musty smell of curing alfalfa. I was back to my childhood on the hay crews. I noticed as I drove on the patchwork quilt of fields that some were green, and others were ripening shades of yellow.

Just before I reached home, I passed through the lava rocks on the Arco desert and caught the distinct smell of rain-soaked juniper and sage. And then I was home, and glad to be there.

I want to remind you of the word of the Lord: "The fullness of the earth is yours," He said. "All things which come of the earth, in the season thereof, are made for the benefit and the use of man, both to please the eye and to gladden the heart. Yea for food and for raiment, for taste, and for smell, to strengthen the body and enliven the soul" (D&C 59:16–19).

I'd like to recommend a road trip! Sure, gas is expensive! But what costs more? Gas, or discouragement, boredom, and misery? The Earth is a gift of joy and life. It's yours. Go get some—now!

ABRAHAM

When the God of heaven refers to a man as His friend, calls him a rock, and commands the rest of us to look to that man and be like him, we should listen. Such a man was Abraham. And his wife, Sarah, was not a whit behind him, for she, too, has been held up to us as an example of faith (see Hebrews 11:11) and of proper conduct (see 1 Peter 3:5–6).

Abraham and Sarah married and wanted children, but children did not come. For decades, the Lord repeatedly promised them children and that their posterity would become as the stars of heaven. Yet, no child came. It would have been so easy to reject those promises when forty years passed without fulfillment.

Then, it ceased to be with Sarah after the manner of women, making the promises of the Lord even more a bitter mockery. And yet, the Lord continued to promise that Sarah would bear a son. Finally, when Abraham was one hundred years old and Sarah ninety, Isaac was born. Can you imagine how time and want had made him so precious to them? They had this miracle boy for not many years, and then came the voice of the Lord.

"Abraham."

Abraham responded, "Here I am."

"Take now thy son, thine only son Isaac, whom thou lovest, and get thee into the land of Moriah; and offer him up there for a burnt offering upon one of the mountains which I shall tell thee of."

Could God have asked of Abraham anything more heartrending than to kill the son of his bosom, a son for whom Abraham had such a love that even God mentions it? And to kill him as a human sacrifice would have been especially repugnant to Abraham who, himself, had once been laid on an altar and nearly sacrificed because of his idolatrous father.

But Abraham raised the knife without hesitation. How could he do that? Long before that knife stood poised to pierce Isaac's heart, Abraham had pierced and broken his own heart. He trusted God more than himself, believed God when it seemed impossible, and obeyed God when he didn't want to. And now, he was willing to give God the most precious thing he possessed if God wanted it, even if the pain in his heart at that moment was worse than that of any knife could ever inflict.

But he was willing. Hence, forever and ever, beyond all doubt by any soul here or in eternity, Abraham proved his greatest love and loyalty.

The angel intervened, Isaac was spared, and Abraham was exalted.

"Now I know," the Lord said, "that thou fearest God, seeing thou hast not withheld thy son, thine only son from me" (Genesis. 22:12).

The Lord has declared that we must be chastened and tried even as Abraham (see D&C 101:4). Most of us live in fear of that day, but remember, long before God asked Abraham to kill Isaac, He asked Abraham to believe. Before God ever commanded him to go to Mount Moriah, He commanded Abraham to leave his home and go to Canaan. Abraham was prepared for that moment when it seemed all eternity was at stake by a lifetime of little choices and silent surrenders when it seemed little was at stake. I declare with soberness that what you do with your heart now will make all the difference in what God can do with you later.

Adapted from Genesis 22.

Hey Diddle, Diddle, and Truth

Hey Diddle Diddle, the cat and the fiddle;
  The cow jumped over the moon.
The little dog laughed to see such sport,
And the dish ran away with the spoon.

Some time ago I happened to be walking through a room, and I overheard my wife reading this nursery rhyme with my daughter, when all of a sudden my daughter, Annie, blurted out, "That is so weird!"

I stopped and turned around. "What's weird?" I asked.

With a tone of ridicule, Annie said, "That book is so weird. Cats can't play the fiddle; cows can't jump over the moon; dogs can laugh,"—I don't know where she got that one—"but dishes do not run away with spoons. That book is just weird!"

Well, she left no doubt by her tone what she thought of the veracity of Mother Goose. But I was taken aback as much by what she said as that she said it in the first place. Annie was only five years old. Evidently, my little girl already recognized that some books are true, and some books are just silly.

Trust me—there's a story here. There is power in truth that steps over the limits of time. Truth is knowledge of things as they are, as they were, and as they are to come. We are beings of truth and light, and the very sum of our mortal existence is to search out truth and improve our intelligence. Where we find truth, we find light. And those who love truth will seek after it and be embraced by those who also love truth.

By the power of the Holy Ghost, we may be guided to the truth of all things and be made free. Indeed, God is God, and He is all-powerful by reason of His knowledge of truth. He lives to give us truth. But truth is so hard for us to bear because it is so hard against sin and error.

And so, herein is the ultimate agency for us: As never before in this world's history, truth blazes around us like the sun at noonday. Will we love it, receive it, live it, and be glorified by it, or will we choose to walk in darkness at noonday, content with cheap fiction and endless entertainment? No wonder we have been encouraged to turn off the television and open up good books. If you really want reality that's real and of eternal worth—truth—go search in the depths where it glittering lies. I promise you, it is a treasure of eternal worth!

A Conversation About Prayer

No man can be saved until he learns to pray. Hence, the commandment to pray is as present in our scriptures as is water on our planet. But will He really answer me, a sinner? Before you set out to converse with the Father, there is another conversation from long ago that you need to overhear.

One night, the Savior went up into a mountain somewhere in Galilee and spent all night in prayer. When it was day, He called His disciples and ordained twelve to be Apostles (see Luke 6:12–13). It appears that He then came down from the mount and found a great multitude waiting for Him on the plain. He ministered to them and then went up into the mountain again. He called His disciples to Him, and in the presence of the people, He began to teach them in preparation for their forthcoming missionary labors (see Luke 6:16–20). Matthew called it the Sermon on the Mount. Luke records it as the Sermon on the Plain.

Near the end, Jesus was instructing His disciples what they should and should not teach the people. He said, "Say unto them, ask of God. Ask and ye shall receive, seek and ye shall find, knock and it shall be opened unto you. For everyone that asketh receiveth, and he that seeketh shall find and to him that knocketh it shall be opened."

But then His disciples, knowing something about the people they were going to teach, said to Him, "They will say unto us . . . God, we know, heard Moses and some of the Prophets; but us He will not hear. And they will say, we have the law for our salvation, and that is sufficient for us" (JST, Matthew 7:14–15).

Does that not sound familiar? "He won't answer us; we're not good enough."

Listen to the Master's reply: "Thus shall ye say unto [the people], what man among you having a son and he shall be standing out, and shall say, Father, open thy house that I may come in and sup with thee, will not say, Come in, my son; for mine is thine, and thine is mine" (JST, Matthew 7:16–17)? "Or what man is there of you, whom if his son ask bread, will he give him a stone? Or if he ask a fish will he give him a serpent? If ye then, being evil, know how to give good gifts unto your children, how much more shall your Father which is in heaven give good things to them that ask Him?" (Matthew 7:9-11).

Could you ever lock your pleading child out of your house? Would you ever deny your children food, no matter what they did?

Neither will He!

"I Am Dry"

The Lord loves and is aware of the missionaries who have been called to preach His gospel. He has promised, "I will go before your face. I will be on your right hand and on your left, and my Spirit shall be in your hearts, and mine angels round about you, to bear you up" (D&C 84:88).

In the Central States Mission in 1926, Elder John Johansen and his missionary companion, Elder Alma Redding, saw the hand of the Lord protect them. In late afternoon as they were tracting in rural Isanti County, Minnesota, a thunderstorm threatened the area.

The elders went to the first house, where a man refused to listen to them or allow them any shelter from the storm. At a second house, the owners were busily rushing through their chores and sharply answered the elders, refusing them any shelter from the storm. Continuing the long walk through the field to the third home, the elders received the same rejection.

As the wind blew and the rain came down in torrents, their pathway down the road was lit by bolts of lightning. They shouldered their bags and continued down the road, unprepared and unprotected. Seemingly abandoned and alone, the elders knelt on the side of the road and petitioned the Lord for help.

Elder Redding later wrote of this night in a letter to John:

"Is there a God? Yes. Does He hear and answer prayers? Yes. Will He watch and protect His servants while they are proclaiming His gospel message to the inhabitants of the earth? Yes.

"Were we unprotected that night? NO! It was a most remarkable experience as we arose, took our country bags, and walked down the road in the midst of the storm, with water dripping from our cases and falling on all sides of us. You uttered, 'Elder Redding, I'm dry.' Then upon looking myself over, I exclaimed, 'So am I.'

"I was in tears as I uttered those words.

"No greater happiness can come to a man than to reach up in the heavens and have God grasp his hand and witness to him that his mission is accepted."

Story Contributed by Jean Tonioli.

Jaxson and Blair

It was once said by a wise man that more religion is caught than taught. I think I believe that. The Apostle Paul said we should be "an example of [all] the believers" (1 Timothy 4:12) You just never know who's watching.

One morning before kindergarten, six-year-old Jaxson came to his mother and asked if he could do his own hair that day. Normally Mom helped him. I suppose she'd seen a few hairstyles in her days done by six-year-olds. But for some reason, that day she said he could go ahead. Oh, he was so excited! He ran in and got in front of the mirror, and he went to work. He was gone for about thirty minutes.

Several times he came to his mother to have her inspect his work. At one point she said, "Okay, you can stop. It looks good."

But Jaxson wasn't satisfied. Back to the mirror he went. Finally, he came out and announced that he was done. "Mom," he said, "how does my hair look?"

"It looks great," Mom said, and it did.

"Are you sure?" Jaxson pressed.

"Yes," Mom assured him.

Then to Mom's surprise, Jaxson asked her to come with him. Well, she was busy at the moment; she tried to put him off. But Jaxson wouldn't hear of it. "Come right now, Mom" he insisted.

She followed him into the hallway where all the family pictures were hanging. He pointed up to the senior picture of his older brother, Blair.

"Mom," he said, "does my hair look exactly like Blair's?"

"It does," she said. "You did so good."

Then touching the front of his hair, he asked, "Even the part right here?"

Even the part was right.

You know, what touched me about this story was that Mom told it just days before Blair left to serve in Toronto, Canada, for two years. Who can measure the impact that Blair's service will have on that adoring younger brother?

It is a compliment of the highest order to be emulated by others. It is not an overstatement to say that there has been, and will yet be, many souls saved in the kingdom of heaven because the simple, unpretentious obedience of one lead another to find his master.

I am one who was led by the light of another. I know it's true. Let your light so shine.

Experience related by Joni Archibald.

Nothing to Fear

Not too long ago, I came around a corner on a quiet Wyoming highway, and there were some horses all bunched up and running. I looked to see why, and there was a small dog chasing them. He couldn't have weighed more than ten pounds, but he had that whole herd of horses on the run. It was a comical sight to see all those great, big horses running from one little spit of a mutt!

I wonder how many of us are afraid when we don't need to be and are running when we don't have to, scared of our own shadows. How many of us worry ourselves into a lather? Confidence before God and man comes with who and what you know.

Years ago, while I was serving as a missionary, I was walking one evening to an appointment with a new partner. The week before, we had met a group of wild teenagers involved in some pretty extreme behavior—you know what I mean. We sat down to teach them, and tact had never been my talent. So, I managed to offend them with my bluntness. Consequently, the next week they were angry and intent on hurting us at our next appointment.

We were walking up the hill that evening toward their house, and we heard this loud awful music—the kind that resembles the noise of a railroad-switching yard. My new companion pointed up the hill to this rundown house, and he said, "Man, I'm sure glad we don't have to go there!"

With some dismay on my face as I realized where the music was coming from, I said, "That's where we're going!" Ah, the look on his face was a Kodak moment.

We came to the door, we knocked, and the gang leader met us at the door wearing dark glasses. It was nighttime. His look of menace and the dim candles heightened the sense of evil. Don't ask me why, but we went in. The entire gang was seated around the room, all glaring at us and all wearing dark glasses. We sat down expecting the worst.

"Okay—teach us," the leader sneered.

I looked up at my companion, and to this day I don't know what came over me. I should have run. But then again, maybe I do know what came over me. Did I mention to you that my companion that night was an Olympic-class swimmer? He stood six-foot-six, weighed more than two hundred and fifty pounds, and was all tone and muscle. I felt no fear, only anger.

I told them what I thought of their heavy-handed intimidation when all of a sudden my big companion cut me off, and he took over on them. And they really listened when he went after them. And before long, the mood in that room mellowed. They turned off the music, and they turned on the lights, and all of a sudden, we were friends again. We never saw a conversion in those knot-heads' lives, but they were always our friends after that.

Now, the bigger and tougher your friends, the easier it is to have confidence. That is precisely why the Lord repeatedly reminds us, "Fear not, I am with thee" (Isaiah 41:10).

He called Himself our rearward, meaning, "I will guard your back; I've got your back" (see Isaiah 52:12; Isaiah 58:8).

We will have perfect confidence before God and men when we have perfect love for Him and our neighbors. That kind of love takes time and practice, but when your conscience is clear, there is nothing to fear.

Bartimaeus the Blind Beggar

To those who are prisoners—those who are caught and bound by circumstances not of their choosing—there is a man in the scriptures I would like you to meet. His name is Bartimaeus.

On the Savior's final journey to Jerusalem, He passed through Jericho. As He came out with a large group of people, He passed by a man sitting like pitiful litter on the side of the road. It was the blind beggar, Bartimaeus.

Hearing a commotion, Bartimaeus asked what was happening. When he learned that Jesus of Nazareth was passing by, hope surged like a shock through him. Suddenly, he became animated and cried with a loud voice, "Jesus, thou Son of David have mercy on me."

Those with Jesus rebuked Bartimaeus and told him to hold his peace. But Bartimaeus would not be deterred. He only cried out louder.

To his fellows, Bartimaeus was an irritation and an interruption, but to Jesus, he was like a crying child. The Savior stopped and commanded him to be brought.

Now those around Bartimaeus cared. "Be of good comfort," they said, "rise, He calleth thee."

Bartimaeus then threw off his garment and went to Jesus. Who can even imagine his excitement? Why does it matter to Mark, the gospel writer, that the garment was thrown off? Because this was the depth of Bartimaeus's faith. Have you ever noticed the clothing of a beggar? It's not usually our fashion of choice. The garment, like the man, would not be the latest fashion, but rather a cast-off, tattered and forgotten. To cast off his old garment was to cast off his old life.

With earnest compassion the Master asked, "What wilt thou that I should do unto thee?"

Somehow word of the Healer had before reached Bartimaeus. From those wind-borne seeds, faith blossomed, nurtured by the pain of his personal bondage. Blindness was his prison. Sight would be new life.

"Lord, that I might receive my sight," he pleaded.

"Go thy way," Jesus said to him, as He touched his eyes. "Thy faith hath made thee whole."

And Bartimaeus saw. Now, free at last to see his own way, Bartimaeus went instead the Master's way. And what way was that? The ascending road from Jericho to Jerusalem, where the mists of darkness have so blinded minds and hardened hearts that the Light of the World will die on Calvary's Hill.

Just as there are none so blind as those who will not see, so, too, there are none so bound as those who bind themselves. But no prison is ever permanent when there is faith in the Savior. If you are that prisoner, have you had enough? If so, cry unto Him for mercy. Be patient in pain until it's time, for that pain can purify your soul and prepare your faith. And then, when He visits you, throw off your past like filthy, disgusting clothing. Remember that agency may have put you in prison, but in Christ no prison is permanent.

Zacchaeus in riches came out of a tree, Bartimaeus in rags out of a gutter, set free—that day in Jericho I long to see.

Asleep at the Concert

Jesus taught His disciples, "No man knoweth the Son, but the Father; neither knoweth any man the Father, save the Son, and they to whom the Son will reveal Himself; they shall see the Father also" (JST, Matthew 11:27). To truly know Jesus Christ, His life must be revealed to us. We can't truly know just by reading about Him. We have to experience His life through our own.

A famous philharmonic orchestra once came to our area. We went as a family because we have two beautiful daughters who love music. The star performer was a young violinist of some accomplishment. He played a concerto piece from Tchaikovsky. He was good—very good, as were they all. At one point in the performance, I looked around. Everyone seemed enthralled by the music. At the end, the audience awarded him ovation after ovation. I can't remember an audience lauding such a performance as they did his.

And where was I in all this commotion and rejoicing? The clapping woke me up. I was fighting sleep. I'm sure that the good people around me wondered what my problem was.

I've wondered since then, *what is my problem?* I knew it was good. I knew I was seeing talent. I knew they were doing something quite difficult. So how could I fall asleep?

Because I share no experience with music. I do not play any musical instruments. I have never given myself to the hours of practice that it takes to perfect an instrument. I can't read music, not a note. I have never paid the least price to make music. I cannot fully appreciate what I have not experienced. On the other hand, those who have lived, suffered, and loved music knew and appreciated the difficulty of his performance, and their response was moving and emotional. They saw his music through their own.

The Savior's life was a masterpiece that only those who have tried to be like Him can fully appreciate. In loving our enemies, the Spirit helps us see how He loved His. When we hurt so much that we cannot bear that someone else suffer as we do, we then see why He went about doing good. When we carry someone else and suffer because of them unto death, we glimpse what Gethsemane was like for Him. We see His life through our own. We know Him as live in Him.

Stillman Pond

I don't suppose that I'm alone when I say that sometimes life gets pretty difficult. And I also have learned from past experience that when life seems difficult, sometimes it helps to hear about someone who has had it a little rougher than you. With that in mind, I'd like to share a story of a pioneer named Stillman Pond.

Stillman Pond and his family were among the last to leave Nauvoo in September 1846. Having already endured much persecution and harassment from enemies, the Pond family was ultimately driven from their home at the point of a bayonet. Without adequate preparation for their trek, they left without proper food, clothing, and shelter. Across Iowa they journeyed, and it was fraught with almost unimaginable suffering and heartache.

Snow came early to Iowa Territory that year, making travel even that much more difficult. Weakened from trudging through the deep snow, Stillman's pregnant wife, Maria, who had already been afflicted with consumption, then contracted malaria. She, along with every member of her family, suffered greatly from this sickness. Bowed with grief and aching from the pain and fever of malaria, Maria could no longer walk. Amidst these grim circumstances she gave birth to twin boys. They both died only a few days later. The deaths of these children coming across the plains from Nauvoo to Winter Quarters were only the beginning of the sacrifice and trials of Stillman Pond.

With all of the members of the Pond family now sick with malaria, Stillman, who was himself unable to walk or even sit up, lay on his stomach in the bed of his wagon; bracing himself with one arm and extending his other over the dashboard to hold the reins, he drove his team the last 150 miles. On October 16, 1846, they arrived at Winter Quarters.

During that winter, the Pond family continued to suffer. In the space of five days, three more children died. A sixth died a few weeks later.

Laura Jane Pond, age fourteen, died of "chills and fever" on December 2, 1846.

Harriet M. Pond, age eleven, died "with chills" on December 4.

Abigail A. Pond, age eighteen, "died with chills" on December 7.

Lyman Pond, age six, died with "chills and fever" on January 15, 1847.

Having survived the heartache of burying all her children, the hardships of the trek across Iowa, and the hunger and privations of a long, hard winter, Stillman's beloved wife, Marie, finally succumbed to her sickness on May 17 at Winter Quarters. Yet despite all of this, Stillman Pond journeyed onward, arriving in the Salt Lake Valley in the early fall of 1847. His testimony of the gospel, his faith in the Lord Jesus Christ, and the fire of the covenant that burned in his soul gave him the strength to go on.

My dear friends, may it be so with us.

Sources:
Leon Y. Pond and H. Ray Pond, "Stillman Pond: A Biographical Sketch," typescript copy, LDS Historical Department, 4–5.

Brent L. Top, *It Still Takes Faith*, BYU Devotional Assembly, July 22, 1997, 2–3.

Blizzards of Experience

Life is a journey, and heaven is a real destination. There is only one road home to the Father, and that road is straight—in other words, it's tight, and it's restrictive. That road is surely a scenic byway and a great adventure, but it is not casual traveling.

Late one night as I was traveling home from Salt Lake City to Idaho, I ran into snow. As I went north, the snow became heavier until it was a blizzard, and then it was a whiteout. Huge wet flakes driven by wind obliterated the painted lines and the road markers. I went slower and slower until I was barely moving. I couldn't stop, but I also couldn't move. It was a maelstrom of swirling white. I couldn't tell where the road was. In fact, the front of my car suddenly dipped out from under me, and I knew I'd driven off the road. I corrected quickly. There seemed to be millions of flashes of reflective white lights streaming at high speed into my windshield, blurring my vision and spinning my head. It seemed never to end, mile after mile.

Every car that I saw that night passed me. I tried, but I could not keep up with them. How could they go so fast in such a storm? But doggedly, I kept going, gauging where I was on the road by the reflector posts on the side of the road. With the gutter on my left and rumble strip on my right, I went up and over Malad Pass, leaving a track that would have resembled the waddle of a drunken duck.

Finally, after some fifty miles, the storm cleared, and I stopped for a break. I walked around the front of my car and did a double take at my headlights. They were packed with snow! I had come all the way through that storm with no headlights. No wonder I couldn't keep up! Running a blizzard at night is crazy enough, but going it with my own lights dimmed, well, that's just dumb! That was the worst blizzard I have ever experienced.

Jesus has already traveled the entire road from heaven to hell and back again. He ascended to the highest heights and descended to the lowest depths. No one knows the road of human experience better than He does.

Jesus commanded us to "abide in Him." *Abide* means, "He's our home; we live in Him permanently; we live for Him." But He also said that as we traveled the journey of mortality, we would be called to pass through tribulation. Do you see the difference? Misery comes when we get that mixed up.

We are to abide in Christ and pass through tribulation, not pass through Christ as though he's a weigh-station and a road sign and then abide in tribulation. To pass through Christ is to ever and always abide in trouble; the storms will never end. There are too many of us that dwell on our problems and live in them, rather than living in Christ and letting the problems pass.

I promise if you will abide in Christ, tribulation will always pass; moreover, it will pass through you—making you wiser, smarter, and stronger. It will always end, my friend, in a small moment. The Master will see to that.

You know that tribulation and opposition in mortality are gifts. They teach wisdom; they teach virtue. Jesus could not have been the Christ without the experience of tribulation, opposition, and pain.

Can any less be asked of you?

Hannah and Samuel

For me, the Old Testament story of Hannah and Samuel embodies the real spirit of motherhood.

Hannah considered herself a woman greatly afflicted. She was barren, unable to bear children. And though her husband loved her dearly and treated her well, still there was an ache in her heart that only a child could fill and God could understand.

One day on an excursion to the temple at Shiloh, Hannah went before the Lord in fasting and prayer. The record says, "she was in bitterness of soul, and prayed unto the Lord, and wept sore" (1 Samuel 1:10).

So anxious was she to bear a child that in her prayer "she vowed a vow, and said, O Lord of hosts, if thou wilt indeed look on the affliction of thine handmaid, and remember me, and not forget thine handmaid, but wilt give unto thine handmaid a man child, then I will give him unto the Lord all the days of his life" (1 Samuel 1:11).

As Hannah prayed, Eli, the priest, watched her. He came over to her, and she poured out the anguish of her heart. As the Lord's representative and moved by the Spirit of God, Eli gave Hannah a promise, saying, "Go in peace: and the God of Israel grant thee thy petition that thou hast asked of him" (1 Samuel 1:17).

Hannah was a woman of great faith. With that promise secure in her heart, she went on her way rejoicing and at peace. Not long after, true to that promise, Hannah conceived and bore a son and called his name Samuel, which interestingly enough means "heard of God."

For three years after that, Hannah refused to leave Samuel and leave home. She was attentive to his every need. Then came the day that must have rent her soul. After the appropriate sacrifices were offered, she presented him to Eli at the temple, saying, "my lord, I am the woman that stood by thee here, praying unto the Lord. For this child I prayed; and the Lord hath given me my petition which I asked of him: Therefore also I have lent him to the Lord; as long as he liveth he shall be lent to the Lord" (1 Samuel 1:26–28). And so it was.

Samuel became a mighty prophet in Israel. And Hannah, that wonderful woman who had craved so dearly the privilege of being a mother, was blessed for her faithfulness with three more sons and two daughters. God keeps His promises.

Thank God for those women today, though declining in numbers, who still yearn to be mothers—who still pray to the God of Israel for the privilege of bearing children, who still refuse to leave them for other pursuits, whose hearts are still rent by the great sacrifice of giving them up to the service of the Lord. They will, like Hannah, change history, and heaven will honor them forever and ever.

Dates with Destiny

I care not for any theory that makes me an evolutionary end product, a random accident of nature, or some kind of mutated monkey.

My friends, we are the children of God, born of love with purpose in our being. The day of our birth, our life's mission, and the day of our death are planned and prepared by our loving Father. And all of His designs are for our greatest happiness. Yet sometimes we fail to recognize that the obstacles of our present course can be a shadowed pathway to greatness. And if we're not careful, we may in our kicking and floundering ruin heaven's plans for us. The Almighty has given us that privilege.

This reminds me of a very talented young man many years ago who almost missed his eternal appointment. You see, he was elected to Congress at the tender age of thirty-two, becoming its second youngest member. He quickly distinguished himself in what were then very turbulent times. Congress adjourned, and he went home for much-needed rest. But while at home, tragedy stuck. His eighteen-month-old daughter, Jane, suddenly died. Stricken with grief, he returned with a heavy heart to his duties in Congress.

His wife, however, became very low until he begged leave to go home and care for her. He worried about her constantly. As he made preparations to return to Congress, his mother died unexpectedly at the age of fifty-seven. Now the weight of it all reduced him, and he was incapacitated for weeks with terrible headaches.

After he returned to Congress, he learned that his home state of Virginia was writing a new constitution. Considering that that was a work of greater import than anything going on in Congress, he wanted to be there. There was perhaps no man more qualified with learning, truth, and pen to contribute to such an undertaking as Virginia's new constitution. He tried to get himself called home to participate, but no invitation was forthcoming. So, he reluctantly remained behind in Congress, worried about his ailing wife but attentive to his responsibilities. And well for us that he did.

You see, within just a few weeks, this junior member of Congress would be called on to speak for his country in her greatest national decision. He would write these words:

"These united colonies are and of a right ought to be free and independent states."

It was the Declaration of Independence—and that reluctant Congressman was Thomas Jefferson. No one in 1776, including Mr. Jefferson, had any idea how deeply his eloquence would change this world.

And so, my friends:

"If ever I become too stubborn about where I want to be,

"I may miss that choice position once ordained for me."

Following Porcupines

A long time ago the Lord said through Isaiah, "Hearken unto me ye that follow after righteousness, look unto the rock from whence ye are hewn and to the hole of the pit from whence ye are digged. Look unto Abraham your father and unto Sarah, she that bare you; for I called him alone and blessed him" (Isaiah 51:1–2). As modern chips off an ancient block, are we as dedicated to following the Lord as was Abraham?

Years ago, I had a wildlife behavior class in college. For a semester project, two of us decided to study the foraging patterns of porcupines. Don't laugh. We considered it cutting-edge science.

We drove up into the mountains and found a porcupine in a tree. We shook him out of the tree and caught him with my coat. Pincushion doesn't even describe what my coat resembled.

Porky then hit the ground and took off running. We ran him down and, by a trick I don't recommend you try at home, we picked him up, flipped him over, and dusted his belly with luminescent powder.

With practice we got pretty good at this. Our worst encounter was my friend getting a quill buried in his leg that came out the other side months later.

After the dusting, we let him go and came back that night with a portable black light. We followed his shining blue trail over the snow, mapping everywhere he went and what he did. Can you just picture it—two grown men following a dumb porcupine in the middle of the night, sometimes on their hands and knees, through deep snow, to learn what he finds interesting? I can tell you, chubby porcupines can crawl through some pretty tight places.

We did this sleep-depriving project for weeks. At the semester's end, we put all our data together and learned . . . nothing! We could find no pattern to how a porcupine eats or travels. He goes where he wants, when he wants, and winds up absolutely wherever he feels like. He is a creature of whim with no purpose higher than his appetites. I still laugh at myself over that venture.

Most people of this world are no more worth following than a hungry porcupine, for the same reason. They are not going where you want to go.

Follow the Lord Jesus Christ. He is the only way to permanent happiness. Don't give up. Those few who firmly follow Jesus take flight with eagles while the many grub with porcupines and go nowhere.

Honor Thy Mother

Learning to honor our parents is so important that God made it a part of the Ten Commandments. If one cannot honor earthly parents who he can see, how can he honor heavenly parents who he can't see? We well know how Jesus honored His Father throughout His life, but what of the Savior's relationship with His mother? How did He treat her?

At the age of twelve, Jesus traveled with His family from Nazareth to Jerusalem for one of the biggest celebrations of the year, the Feast of the Passover. As this feast concluded and the tens of thousands of pilgrims started for home, Joseph and Mary did likewise, joining with the company in traveling north out of Jerusalem about a day's journey. They had supposed that Jesus was somewhere in the caravan. But at day's end when they went looking for Him, they soon discovered He was not there; Jesus was nowhere to be found. Can you imagine Joseph and Mary's feelings? "Oh dear, we've lost the Son of God!"

They went back a day's journey to Jerusalem, and after three days found Him sitting in the temple listening to the teachers there. They were, as you can imagine, justifiably distraught. "Son," Mary says, "why hast thou thus dealt with us?" (Luke 2:48). There's no mistaking the chiding in her voice.

"How is it that ye sought me?" Jesus replies. "[Know] ye not that I must be about my Father's business?" (Luke 2:49).

It's interesting that the scripture records that Joseph and Mary did not understand what He meant by that statement.

We have here a most unique situation. Probably for the first time in history, we actually do have a child who is in all ways smarter than His parents. He is the most intelligent being on the planet, capable, if you will, of governing the kingdom of the Jews if He were simply old enough. So how is He going to react toward His parents? He could have said, "I know what I'm doing; stop treating me like a child." Or He could have said something like this: "Dad, Mom, sit down before you hurt yourself." Or He could have acted in any number of inappropriate ways toward His parents, but He didn't.

Listen to what the scriptural record says: "he went down with them, and came to Nazareth, and was subject unto them" (Luke 2:51).

Jesus gave the law, "Honour thy Father and [thy] Mother" (Exodus 20:12), and when His mortal test came, He fulfilled that law perfectly. It is well to note that He honored His earthly parents not necessarily because they earned it, but because it was His duty.

It is just as much a commandment for children to honor their parents as it is for parents to teach the gospel to their children. To honor our parents is to honor God. After all, children, it was He who called them to their position, not you.

Based on Luke 2.

Gnat on My Pillow

On a recent Saturday morning I woke up slowly. The morning light was streaming through the window. I opened my eyes, and there was a gnat only a fraction of an inch from my face. He was so close to the end of my nose, but so small that I could barely see him. He was there for only a fraction of a second, and then he was gone! Many people don't even think at that time of the morning, but for some reason my brain kicked into gear.

That's me, I thought to myself. *That's how I feel—like that gnat—so insignificant. I'm nothing! I'm here one minute, and then I'm gone forever the next. And what will I leave behind so someone will know that I was ever here? Will this world even know or care that Glenn Rawson existed?*

I thought about that gnat all day long, and it hammered on my mind. I don't want to live and die a gnat!

I believe I'm not the only child of the Almighty who feels this way.

Moses had been a Prince of Egypt, a mighty in power in the court of Pharaoh. He gave it up. He fled into the wilderness of Sinai, and he became a shepherd. And then one day the Lord called Moses up into the mountain, and while the glory of God was upon him, Moses spoke with God face to face.

"I have a work for thee, Moses my son;" the Father said, "and thou art in the similitude of mine Only Begotten" (Moses 1:6).

He then showed Moses great visions that caused Moses to marvel and to wonder—such things as he had never imagined! When the Lord withdrew from Moses, he fell to the earth and for many hours had not enough strength to even stand up.

In this exhausted state, Moses reflected to himself, "Now, for this cause I know that man is nothing, which thing I never had supposed" (Moses 1:10).

And there is the burning question: Is man "nothing" or is he a child of God and "a little lower than the angels" (Hebrews 2:6–7; Psalms 8:4–5)? Is he less than the dust of the earth or more precious than fine gold? Which is it?

The answer: We are both.

To God, we are His children of infinite worth and precious in His sight. But before God and His power, might, majesty, and glory, we are nothing in comparison. In our fallen state, we are worthless (see Mosiah 4:5).

All of us are indeed as gnats—until we recognize our fallen mortal condition and our everlasting dependence on the Almighty. When Moses the shepherd came to this knowledge, he became Moses the great deliverer. All of us would do well to wake up as did Moses and know where we stand before the Almighty. In the words of Neal A. Maxwell, "we do not stand . . . We kneel!" ("O, Divine Redeemer," *Ensign*, November 1981).

"In His Presence"

About 73 B.C., Alma the Younger, caught in the agony of his many sins, suddenly cries out in his heart, "O Jesus, thou Son of God have mercy on me." As soon as he cried out, "I could remember my pains no more; yea, I was harrowed up by the memory of my sins no more. And, oh what joy and what marvelous light I did behold; yea, my soul was filled with joy as exceeding as was my pain." He saw God sitting on His throne and, "my soul did long to be there," he said.

In the Spring of 1820, young Joseph Smith stood in the presence of the Father and the Son and conversed with them. Later he would describe the experience, "My soul was filled with love and for many days I could rejoice with great joy and the Lord was with me."

In the School of the Prophets meetings in the winter of 1833, John Murdock describes the following:

> The Prophet told us if we could humble ourselves before God, and exercise strong faith, we should see the face of the Lord. And about midday the visions of my mind were opened, and the eyes of my understanding were enlightened, and I saw the form of a man, most lovely, the visage of his face was sound and fair as the sun. His hair a bright silver gray, curled in most majestic form. His eyes a keen penetrating blue, and the skin of his neck a most beautiful white and he was covered from the neck to the feet with a loose garment, pure white, whiter than any garment I have ever before seen. His countenance was most penetrating, and yet most lovely. And while I was endeavoring to comprehend the whole personage from head to feet it slipped from me, and the vision was closed. . . . But it left on my mind the impression of love, for months, that I never felt before to that degree.

About 1918, Elder Melvin J. Ballard was given a dream or vision of the Savior in the temple. He described it as follows:

> As I entered the room I saw, seated on a raised platform, the most glorious being I have ever conceived of, and was taken forward to be introduced to Him. As I approached, He smiled, called my name, and stretched out His hands towards me. If I live to be a million-years-old I shall never forget that smile. He put His arms around me and kissed me, as He took me into His bosom, and He blessed me until my whole being was thrilled. As He finished, I fell at His feet, and there saw the marks of the nails; and as I kissed them, with deep joy swelling through my whole being, I felt that I was in heaven indeed.
>
> The feeling that came to my heart then was: Oh! If I could live worthy, though it would require four-score years, so that in the end when I have finished, I could go into His presence and receive the feeling that I then had in His presence, I would give everything that I am or ever hope to be!

And these are just a few examples we could cite of those who have stood in the presence of God and described it. Is it any wonder then that in 3 Nephi 17, when Jesus announced He must leave, "Behold, they were in tears and did look steadfastly upon Him as if they would ask Him to tarry a little longer with them." They could not bear the pain of being away from Him.

And lastly, the disciples of Jesus were journeying and "united in mighty prayer and fasting" when the Savior showed Himself to them. Many things were discussed and taught, but then, Jesus said to them, "What is it that ye desire of me, after that I am gone to the Father?" Evidently, nine of the Twelve knew exactly what they wanted and did not hesitate: "We desire that after we have lived unto the age of man, that our ministry, wherein thou hast called us, may have an end, that we may come speedily unto thee in thy kingdom."

Of all the things they could have asked for, the thing they wanted most was to be with Him. What is heaven? It is where God is. It is what God is. The greatest of all the eternal gifts of God is to be with Him, with our families forever. I'm not sure that we can comprehend the awesome power of standing worthy in the Lord's presence, but I want to.

Alma 36.

https://www.josephsmithpapers.org/paper-summary/history-circa-summer-1832/3.

https://www.ldsscriptureteachings.org/2016/12/09/john-murdock-sees-the-savior/

Melvin J. Ballard—Crusader for Righteousness, 1966, 65–66; M. Russell Ballard, "The Blessings of Sacrifice," Ensign, May 1992, 75.

3 Nephi 17:5.

3 Nephi 27–28.

Hezekiah and Grace

The more you know about the Savior, the more you will love Him, trust Him, and rely on Him.

Hezekiah of the Old Testament became king of Judah at age twenty-five. Immediately he set about to bring his people back to God. He cleansed the temple, restored the dignity of the priesthood, and brought the people together in worship. It was said of him, "in every work that he began . . . to seek his God, he did it with all his heart and he prospered" (2 Chronicles 32:21). He was a righteous man and a credit to his mother, Abi (see 2 Kings 18:2, 5).

But then his people were attacked by the Assyrians. The conquering army swept into Judea and conquered forty-one cities, even besieging Jerusalem itself.

"Be strong and courageous," Hezekiah said to his frightened people, "be not afraid nor dismayed . . . for there be more with us than with him" (2 Chronicles 32:7). And his people believed and "rested themselves upon [his] words" (2 Chronicles 32:8).

All the kingdom sat upon Hezekiah—all the people of God looked to him. Even God and His prophet Isaiah recognized Hezekiah's authority and power as Judah's king. He bore the tremendous weight of a terrible situation.

And then it happened—as if the threats of his enemies were not already enough, Hezekiah got sick (see Isaiah 38:12). It weakened and wore him down to his bed. Isaiah came and announced, "Thus saith the Lord, set thine house in order: for thou shalt die"(Isaiah 38:1).

That proclamation broke Hezekiah's heart. Turning his face to the wall, he prayed and wept, "O Lord, I am oppressed; undertake for me" (Isaiah 38:14).

If it ever should happen that you stand where Hezekiah stood, surrounded, alone, worn down and weary, sick, and utterly powerless to help yourself, know that Jesus is full of grace and truth (see John 1:14). He it is who comes and saves in mortal dilemmas now and eternal damnations later.

The Lord heard Hezekiah immediately and turned Isaiah around to give the humble Hezekiah fifteen more years of life as well as deliverance from Assyria. To the astonishment of all history, the setting sun even rose back into the sky for a sign of comforting proof to this favored son. The Lord was kind to Hezekiah. By the grace of the Almighty, Hezekiah lived on to greatness.

But grace is not just what Jesus gives, it is what He is. It is His nature to help the helpless, love the lonely, free the prisoner, and save the lost. When all you are facing are walls, look up!

Grateful for Gratitude

We are commanded, my friends, to live in thanksgiving daily, always returning thanks for whatsoever we receive. Why? Does God need our gratitude? No, we do.

I will never forget the Christmas of 2006. Shaina wanted a keyboard for Christmas.

I mean, she really wanted a keyboard! We looked at used ones, but the cost was too much. Every chance she got, though, Shaina played one and just dreamed. As young ones do, she pestered us incessantly about wanting a keyboard.

Finally, I sat her down and I explained, "We just can't afford it." But then I said, "Be patient, though, my dear, and I promise I'll get you one. All good things come to those who wait."

She never said another word about it, but we knew she was mightily disappointed. Then for some reason, we felt as though we should make the sacrifice and get it for her. We did.

On Christmas morning we opened our presents, but the keyboard was hidden away. Shaina seemed content and happy with what she'd received, and I noticed that.

Then when all the presents were opened, Mom led the family into the laundry room. There was the prized drum set for Hannah, the guitar for Travis and Sherise, and the keyboard for Shaina.

Hannah screamed and danced through the house. Travis and Sherise picked up the guitar and began to "plink." But Shaina took one look at the keyboard, screamed with excitement, and then turned and buried her face in my chest, just holding on to me. At first, I thought she was laughing. Then I realized she was crying—not just crying, but sobbing with joy. For a long moment she just held on to me and cried and cried and cried. No one noticed, but Dad was crying too, as I do every time I think about that moment. I'm not sure there's anything a father appreciates more than a truly grateful child. Her tears of gratitude were more than ample payment for our sacrifice.

"God so loved the world, that he gave his only begotten Son" (John 3:15).

Just imagine the joy the Father and the Son will share with us when we with true understanding fall at their feet and bathe those feet with tears of joy and gratitude. That child who seeks to understand what has been done for him, and never stops expressing it, is the child that a parent loves to bless.

So, practice your gratitude like Shaina practices piano. It is music to our Father and is the mark of a cultivated mind. To perfect gratitude is to master the natural man and to know God.

Joseph's Dream

For any of you who have ever felt overwhelmed and under-capable—if "deep water is what [you too are] wont to swim in"—then this story is for you.

A man once had a dream where he found himself "standing on a peninsula in the midst of a vast body of water where there appeared to be a large harbor or pier for boats to come to." He was surrounded by his friends. Presently, a strong wind came up that increased into a raging storm, making the waters very rough. A ship began to leave the harbor and make its way "out into the channel."

The man turned to his friends and warned them "that if they did not understand the Signs of the Times and the Spirit of Prophecy, they would be apt to be lost."

Within moments, they witnessed the violent waves break over the departing ship. It "soon foundered and went down with all on board."

The man declared to his friends that he believed he could best those waves and beat the storm. They laughed at him and said he would drown.

"The waters looked clear and beautiful" he said, "though exceedingly rough; and I said I believed I could swim, and I would try it anyhow." They told him again he would drown.

Well, if was going to drown, then he would have fun in the water first, and with that he dove into the "raging waves."

He had not gone far when a towering wave overwhelmed him, but he soon found himself on top of it. Then another wave broke over him and he topped it also.

"I struggled hard," he said, "to live in the midst of the storm and waves, and soon found I gained upon every wave and skimmed the torrent better."

Shortly he discovered that he was able to swim with his head above the waves so that they couldn't break over him. He had swum a great distance and found that he was much enjoying himself. He became stronger and faster until both his head and shoulders were above the water, and he was faster than any ship. The water seemed to calm. His body rose higher and higher until "finally [he] could tread on the top of the water, and went almost with the speed of an arrow."

He thought "it was a great sport and pleasure to travel with such speed," and then he awoke (*History of the Church,* 6:194).

Jesus did many mighty miracles. He walked on water. Do you remember that on the last night of His life, He declared to His disciples, "Verily, verily, I say unto you, he that believeth on me, the works that I do shall he do also; and greater works than these shall he do" (John 14:12)?

We live in the eve of time in a beautiful world fraught with raging storms and violent waves. It is not for us to shrink but to dive in and swim with great determination. The Almighty will help us if we are faithful, until we too can overcome. Look around! According to the signs of the times, it is not the time to whine and worry, but to work.

And by the way, some of you might appreciate knowing what man had that dream. It was a nineteenth-century hero of mine named Joseph Smith.

He Knows Your Name

To those of you who are feeling unloved and insignificant in this big world where love seems to be growing colder, I would like to share some thoughts.

How big is the universe? Estimates are 156 billion light years with some 70 sextillion stars. That is more stars than all the grains of sand on the entire earth.

The sun is ninety-three million miles away and more than ten thousand degrees Fahrenheit. For thousands of years the sun and earth have maintained just the right distance from each other. Imagine global warming if they ever got any closer!

Our earth weighs six sextillion tons. That's a lot of weight! It is an ultra-complex balanced life system nearly eight thousand miles in diameter, and yet more than six billion of us are kept alive by a layer of topsoil only a few feet thick.

The Earth spins around the sun at sixty thousand miles per hour and on its axis at five hundred miles per hour—yet, somehow, I'm not dizzy.

In a universe where distance is measured in light years, consider that all life on only this planet is sustained by an atmosphere only seven miles thick.

And that is only the macro universe—consider the microscopic. An atom, for instance, is so tiny that two billion of them would be needed to make a dot for an *i*. Imagine what would happen if protons and electrons stopped attracting.

Our bodies are a marvel. The human heart is only about the size of a fist, and yet each day it pumps enough fluid to fill a two-thousand-gallon tank. Its valves open and close consistently some one hundred thousand times a day, all using less energy than a small light bulb (Russell M. Nelson, *New Era*, October 1987).

Take a breath. There are about 1,500 miles of airways in your lungs. Your 600 muscles provide the miracle of movement. Nerve signals within the body can travel as fast as 330 feet per second. Your brain is about 3.3 pounds of soggy gray mush, yet within it is the miracle of you. And there are those who think this is all an accident.

All of this wonder since Adam and Eve has begun as the union of two cells. There is order in it all, and it is governed by law. Whether we study through a telescope or a microscope, we are constrained to exclaim, "There is a God, and He is the Creator!" He has all power. None are above Him (see D&C 132:20). All and everything obeys His voice. He is all-knowing. There's not anything save He knows it (see 2 Nephi 9:20). His eye can pierce from the smallest particle to the largest star. He is all-present. From the fall of the sparrow to the sorrow in your heart, He is there and He's aware. He is the great God of the universe!

To paraphrase Elder Neal A. Maxwell, when we consider where we stand before Him, we do not stand at all— we kneel, and that with a profound sense of reverence and awe.

And yet, on that day on Mount Sinai when God appeared to an insignificant Bedouin shepherd, do you remember the first word the Almighty spoke? "Moses" (Exodus 3:4). He called the shepherd by name.

Yes, He knows you, and He knows your name. You are His, and the two of you are well acquainted, and when you see His face again, "nothing is going to startle you more" than just how familiar it is (President Ezra Taft Benson, *Ensign*, December 1988, 6).

Judging Others

Though the Lord Jesus was born after the manner of the flesh, He didn't live after the manner of men. There was nothing coarse or cruel or vulgar or profane about the Lord. He was indeed a pure and a holy man, which makes the events that I'm going to tell you about all the more remarkable.

On a late night in Capernaum when Jesus wanted sleep, multitudes of the needy came to His door. He went out to them, and He healed them (see Mark 1:33–34). When He sought solitude after the death of John, five thousand came, and He welcomed and fed them (see Mark 6:29–44).

It didn't matter whether it was Pharisees or publicans, He dined with them all. Whether it was beggars or blind men, lepers or lame, saints or sinners, all came to Jesus, and all were accepted.

The Savior proved that all men are precious to Him and all are invited to come. None are turned away (see 2 Nephi 26:26). Now, how could one so good be so welcoming and tolerant of those who were not?

When He appeared to His disciples after the Resurrection, there were some who stood doubting and wondering (see John 20:24–27; Matthew 28:16–17). But it didn't matter to Him where they stood or how they felt. All were invited to stand next to Him and feel those sacred wounds.

And again at Bountiful, all were commanded to come unto Him and thrust their hands into His side and feel the prints of the nails in His hands and feet. And one by one, all 2,500 came (see 3 Nephi 11:13–16; 3 Nephi 17:25). And then, one by one He took their sick and their afflicted and healed them—all of them—completely. Then He gathered their children with great tenderness and blessed each one (see 3 Nephi 17:7–12; 21–24).

Their cups were already filled, but the Master wasn't finished yet. He then administered the bread and wine to each of them, inviting each of them present to enter into a sacred covenant relationship with Him (see 3 Nephi 18:1–11).

I marveled for years at the Master's careful attention to detail and to individuals. I believed that that story was written to show us how much He loves us. And then I realized one day that that's true, but there was another reason why Jesus's attention to "one by one" was recorded. At the close of that wonderful day, Jesus said to His Apostles, "ye see that I have commanded that none of you should go away, but rather have commanded that each of you should come unto me that ye [you] might feel and see; even so shall ye do unto the world" (3 Nephi 18:25).

That's it! If you tend to scorn and push others away, please know that you are opening yourself up to temptation—and if you continue, it may be you who is pushed away when you most want acceptance (see D&C 1:10).

Jesus knew all of us, and He feared none of us. His righteousness is greater than our weakness. He is pure and holy, and before Him all of us are unworthy but none of us is unwanted. So it should be with us.

If you have been judged as unworthy and unwanted, it is all right. It hurts—a lot. But let it go. Blessed are ye, for He was there before you, and in an especial way, He will be there for you now (see Matthew 5:10–12).

Patience and the Sons of Thunder

The autumn Feast of Tabernacles was at hand for the Jews. Jesus left Galilee and journeyed to Jerusalem through Samaria. Evidently somewhere toward evening in their travels, they approached a certain village. Jesus sent some disciples on ahead to arrange lodgings for the night. But when the Samaritans realized that Jesus, a Jew, was just passing through on His way to Jerusalem, they were offended, and they refused Him their hospitality. It was a deliberate snub to the Son of God.

The messengers returned to the Savior and informed Him of the rudeness. James and John were standing close behind the Savior, and they heard the report—and they were upset!

"Lord," they said, "wilt thou that we command fire to come down from heaven, and consume them, even as Elias did?" (Luke 9:54).

Jesus turned and rebuked them, saying, "Ye know not what manner of spirit ye are of. For the Son of man is not come to destroy men's lives, but to save them" (Luke 9:55–56).

And with that, Jesus let it go and moved on to another village.

But of what spirit were James and John? I'll tell you. It was the spirit of impatience, indignation, and the desire to hurt—or, in other words, the spirit of evil. James and John, the sons of thunder, were thundering evil at that moment, and they didn't even know it. Surely, they felt that their impatience and indignation were justified, just like we often do. After all, those Samaritans had mistreated the Son of God, their Master! But just imagine where we'd be if God was as short on patience as we often are? Most of us would have been broiled long ago.

Patience is quietness and confidence of soul that yields strength. Patience is part and parcel of faith. Patience is commanded most often in the scriptures in affliction. There is no such thing as long-suffering without patience. It qualifies us to serve the Lord and is a birthmark of the Lord's people. Finally, patience perfects us.

On that day, John the Beloved wanted to destroy those ignorant Samaritans. But as time went on, he would learn from the Master, and later that same John would give new meaning to the term *long-suffering* as he lived and labored to bring a different fire and light to the children of God.

Lastly, and this is most critical: As important as it is to be patient with each other as children of the Lord, it is much more important to be patient with the Lord as His child. After all, you have a long way to go, and He has a lot to do with you.

So, be still, for in patience you may possess your soul; in impatience you will surely throw it away.

Mom and Dad

Love is a gift from God, and men are that they might know love. But we cannot truly love others until we first love God and then feel His love for us. With that, I'd like to share some of my first memories of love.

I was just a little boy growing up in Idaho's Lemhi Valley. Dad was a ranch hand, and Mom stayed at home. I remember Dad going down into the fields to change water and coming back with a bouquet of spring wildflowers for Mom. She would light up like sunshine every time he did that, and he knew she would. The flowers are gone now, but the memories are still there. My dad never knew it, but I was watching.

We were poor growing up, but that didn't seem to matter to Dad at Christmas time. Every year the single most expensive, most thoughtful gift under the tree was the one he got for my mom. And her reaction was always the same. She was thrilled. Somehow it was always the perfect gift, just what she most wanted. She would brag on the gift, and Dad would beam like a lighthouse. They knew how to give and how to receive of each other. My parents really knew how to do Christmas.

I remember another time when my dad made me so angry that I stormed into the house and vented my frustration to my mother. To my surprise, her indignation was instant and fierce. I will never forget how quickly she put me in my place—it was like she body-slammed me! Never again did I speak against my dad to her. No one could come between them. They were one, and they were determined to stay that way. I didn't understand then, but I do now.

I swear, the only thing my mom ever fixed was meat and 'taters. I came to loathe that stuff! Did my mom not know how to cook, you ask? Oh no, my mother is an excellent cook. It's just that meat and 'taters was my dad's favorite meal. She could cook many things, but her favorite thing to fix was what Dad liked.

I still laugh when I remember those times when Dad would sneak up behind my mom, usually while she was cooking, and he would just give her a swat! Mom would whirl around; she'd get all indignant and pretend to be so mad; she'd grab a skillet or anything she could get her hands on and take off after him. Dad would holler and scream like he was being killed, and he would run for his life. She'd always catch him, though—he made sure of that—and they laughed and they tussled, and the outcome was always the same. It always ended in a tender embrace and a kiss. They were the best of friends, and they still are. They have the best marriage this man has ever seen.

My friends, those of you who are loved and in love, be grateful to the God of heaven for this godly gift.

And to those of you whose arms are empty and whose hearts ache, please know that God knows. He is love, and the closer you come to Him, the more you will love and be loved. Those who live with Him and in Him never live alone—not now, not ever!

WHAT MONEY CAN BUY

One day after class, I returned to my office. I was only there a few minutes when I heard the sound of beautiful piano music coming from my classroom. I walked back in, and there was one of my students, a lovely young woman, the mother of two small children and the wife of a hard-working college student.

I was a little surprised. She never spoke in class and she was always content to listen, and she never seemed to draw attention to herself. And yet from those hands poured forth music that was worthy of angels. I complimented her, and I thanked her for playing so well.

She then told me a story I think of often. She told me how she loved the piano and loved to play and had done so for a long time, but she couldn't play much anymore. She didn't own one; they were too poor to afford it. The only opportunity she had to play the piano was when she came to my class.

Ah! What a shame, I thought. Every child needs to hear music such as this. Her family was missing out. What a blessing, what a privilege it would be to have music like that in the home. It would invite the Spirit of the Lord. It would bring peace.

And then I felt something I had never felt before. You know, like everyone else, I had thought *I wish I were a rich man.* But for the first time the feeling came over me that *I wish I were a rich man so I could give it away.*

I would have gone out right then and there and bought that woman a piano worthy of her talent. I would have taken it home and set it up in her small apartment and asked for a concert right in front of her children. But I had no money. I was a teacher, working two jobs as it was. I remember to this day the ache that I couldn't help her, and I wanted to.

That was years ago. I can't remember her name now. But I've never forgotten that ache—wanting to do something good and not having the means to do it. I believe that experience was given to me by my Father in Heaven. It's a worthy scar.

It's fun to have money and buy what you want. But it's joy to have money and help others get what they want. I believe that money matters to the Savior. If it didn't, then why does He always prosper those who keep His commandments? (see Mosiah 2:22). Why are we told of rich young rulers, of camels and the needle's eye? (see Luke 18:25). It matters! The Lord wants all of us to be wise and rich givers.

But there's a paradox. To love money is to die and lose all of it. But to love people with your money is to live and have it all.

May the Lord bless each of us to get rich wisely. May He bless us and help us not to fatten our camels as we do so. By our means, my friend, we may be saved or damned!

I remember a little man in a tree named Zacchaeus (see Luke 19:1–10). God help us to become more like him.

From the experience of Lain Corry Telford.

Plodding

I have to confess that I have been a runner for more than twenty years. And from that passion—or insanity, whichever you call it—I've learned a few lessons.

For example, I've learned about pacing. If I bust out of the house at sunrise feeling all fresh and frisky, and I run too fast, I tire quickly, I lose heart, and it winds up being a short run. But on the other hand, if I don't worry about all the old ladies and the children who are passing me, and I build my speed as I go, I find that I can run for a long time, and I can go a long way. And even more importantly, I love the run—even if I do plod.

Do you know what *plod* means? It means to proceed in a tediously slow manner with constant monotonous perseverance. Therefore, all things considered, I guess you could say I'm more of a plodder than a runner. Besides, at my age, sprinting is just a delusional up-tempo shuffle anyway. To be true and faithful requires pacing.

There was once an ancient prophet who described how his people turned to the grossest sin. They were bloated with pride and ripped apart by contention and war. Mercifully, the Lord did not destroy them—even though they deserved it—but instead He brought down famine that humbled them and gave them the chance to repent. And they did, to the extent that once again this entire nation of people bowed before the Lord and lived in peace with one another.

But here's the hard part: That only lasted about five years, and the people turned like fickle children once again to the addiction of their own egos. Observing this, the prophet wrote of his people, and of human nature in general:

> [T]hus we can behold how false, and also the unsteadiness of the hearts of the children of men . . . at the very time when

the Lord doth prosper His people . . . doing all things for [their] welfare and happiness . . . yea, then is the time that they do forget the Lord their God . . . and do trample under their feet the Holy One. (Helaman 12:1–2)

So, men are by nature not true; we are false, he said—meaning we don't stick, we're not steady, we're not consistent, we don't endure to the end, we fail, we quit, we give up. It's this quality about ourselves, and that we understand it about ourselves, that causes us to tend to revere those who are true and faithful, who stick to great causes at great sacrifice to the very end. We admire them.

Therefore, thanks be to God for such as the Lord Jesus Christ, who didn't quit even though He could; for George Washington and others, who saw the fight through until the ship of state was safe; and for pioneers, who little recognized at the time that their plodding across hostile Wyoming toward a distant hope beyond blue mountains would walk them into history and deep into the affections of our hearts.

July is an interesting month. We are called to remember, and to celebrate our freedom, our heritage, our homes, and our faith. I hope we recognize that these blessings were won by an often-plodding pace of faithfulness, dedication, and obedience. There are too many of us who burst forth with brilliant flashes of faithfulness, followed by fizzle. That will not do in the days ahead. After all, no traveler ever set his course by a falling star.

If you want the promised land, then show God your faith by plodding across your Wyoming. Keep going. Faith is still needed in every footstep. We have a long way to go. Keep the pace and keep the faith. God loves you.

"Oh, It Was Nothing"

It had been a long flight. Mom had left Houston, Texas, early in the morning bound for Idaho, with a layover in Salt Lake. Accompanying her was her four-year-old daughter Annalyn and her two-year-old daughter Abigail. They landed at Salt Lake International in the C concourse, gate one. Their connecting flight was going to take off in forty-five minutes at the E concourse on the other side of the airport—and did I mention that Mom was five months pregnant?

With her two little ones, luggage for all for two weeks, and her other burdens, she hurried across the airport, arriving at her gate with just ten minutes to spare. As she was boarding the aircraft, she suddenly realized that she had left her iPad—her husband's very expensive and very important iPad—in the seat of the previous flight. Seeing the distressed look on her face, the flight attendant asked, "Are you all right?"

With other passengers listening, this young mother explained her dilemma. The flight attendant said, "Well, grab your purse and your ID and run, but I can't promise we'll hold the plane for you."

Mom looked at her and said, "I can't do that." She then asked if there was any way they could contact someone at the other plane. The flight attendant went into the cockpit to confer with the pilots. In a moment she came back and asked which flight she had come in on. She answered and the flight attendant relayed that information to the pilots.

Suddenly the co-pilot bailed out of his seat, and without looking at her or saying a word, did a banister slide down the stairs to the tarmac without touching a single stair. He took off in a sprint in between the parked aircraft and quickly disappeared from view.

In his absence, Mom prayed and agonized. After about ten minutes he came running back, iPad in hand. He boarded the aircraft out of breath amid the cheers of passengers and the relieved tears of my worried daughter, Sherise.

The flight attendant brought the iPad back to Sherise and said with a smile, "You owe that man your life. He just ran all the way to gate C-1 and back."

At the end of the flight in Idaho Falls as Sherise walked up the aisle to get off the plane, First Officer Reed Young was standing there saying goodbye to the passengers. As she approached, Sherise again began to cry. "I don't know how to thank you," she said.

He smiled a big smile, patted her on the arm, and said, "Oh, it was nothing. Have a nice day."

Well, Sir, I beg to differ. Kindness and sacrifice are never nothing. They not only help people have a nice day, but they change lives forever.

The Temptations of Jesus

When Jesus was about thirty years of age[1], He left his family in Nazareth[2] and traveled to the Jordan River to be baptized[3] by John the Baptist. At His baptism, the Holy Ghost descended upon Him like a dove[4], and immediately that Spirit took him into the wilderness[5] to be with God.[6] For forty days, Jesus fasted and communed with Heavenly Father there among the "wild beasts," all the while, Satan, as he always does, "seeking to tempt Him."

At the end of the forty days Jesus was hungry, "and was left to be tempted of the devil."[8] It may seem odd that Heavenly Father would deliberately leave Jesus at such a time as this, but remember, He was spiritually strong, though physically weak.

As it was with Jesus, so it must be with us; we all must be tempted. We all must face good and evil, light and dark, and choose for ourselves. Why? Because no one can appreciate the sweetness of heaven until they have tasted the bitterness of hell.[9]

And this is not a passive process. We are continually being enticed by both sides. While the devil tempts us to indulge in evil, the Spirit of the Lord persuades us to choose good.[10] And choosing righteousness in our weakest moments makes us the strongest.

"If thou be the Son of God," the devil said to Jesus, "command that these stones be made bread."[11] Can you not hear the taunt in his voice?

Why is bread a temptation? Bread is not a sin. Because the sin is not in what is being offered, it is when it is being offered, and by whom, as evidenced by the Savior's answer.

"It is written," Jesus said, "man shall not live by bread alone, but by every word that proceedeth out of the mouth of God."[12] In other words, "I will not partake of bread to end this fast until my Father gives me leave."

So many times, sin is partaking of something good but at the wrong time and in the wrong way. Jesus could wait to feed His starving body. He could wait for power, honor, glory, and kingdoms—until His Father offered them.

By offering us what our body and ego craves now, the devil pulls us away from God and distracts us. Jesus is our example. As we too understand the scriptures and obey the whisperings of the very still, small voice, we come to know what is right and wrong. What remains then is for us to have the courage to tell Lucifer and his helpers where to go. We cannot escape temptation in this life, but, praise God, we can always escape sin.

---

1. Luke 3:23.
2. JST, 3:23.
3. Matthew 3:13.
4. Matthew 3:16.
5. Mark 1:12.
6. Matthew 4:1.
7. Mark 1:13.
8. JST, Matthew 4:2.
9. D&C 29:39.
10. 2 Nephi 2:16.
11. Matthew 4:3.
12. Matthew 4:4.

RUTH

In an age when it seems to be more and more fashionable to be fickle, faithless, and an infidel, there is a story in the Old Testament that is inspiring and refreshing.

During a time of famine in ancient Israel, a man named Elimelech moved his family from Bethlehem to the country of Moab. While there, Elimelech died, leaving behind his wife, Naomi, and two sons. The two sons married Moabite women. It wasn't long before the two sons also died, leaving Naomi alone. Naomi heard that the famine had ended in Israel, and she set her mind to go home. Orpah and Ruth, her two daughters-in-law, went with her.

Somewhere near the border between the two countries, Naomi begged the two girls to go back, to return to their families and make themselves a new life; she had nothing to offer them. Well, after many tears, Orpah kissed Naomi and went back, disappearing into history. Ruth, on the other hand, would not turn back.

"Entreat me not," she said, "to leave thee, or to return from following after thee: for whither thou goest, I will go; and where thou lodgest, I will lodge: thy people shall be my people, and thy God my God: Where thou diest, will I die, and there will I be buried: The Lord do so to me, and more also, if ought but death part thee and me" (Ruth 1:16–17).

Powerful words, but they were not empty drama. In making such a declaration, Ruth would be leaving behind the family of her childhood to follow an impoverished old woman from whom she stood to gain nothing. Ruth would leave behind the country, the customs, and the traditions she had grown up with to enter a strange new land and society that did not always look with favor upon foreigners. And perhaps most significant of all, she would be denouncing the religion and the God of her upbringing for the strange new worship of Jehovah.

Ruth was a virtuous woman filled with faith and loyalty. She stayed with Naomi, and true to her word, Ruth labored to support Naomi and never left her. Then and now, Ruth's loyalty was noticed and honored.

I've thought about this and that quality we call loyalty. Loyalty is a quality stronger than iron in the human soul that binds us to causes, promises, country, spouse, and family. It holds us firmly in that place where we committed ourselves to be, especially when there's no other reason to stay other than "we ought to." History will always honor those loyal to the last measure for true causes. And in that spirit, Ruth was no exception. For her undying loyalty and devotion, Ruth would find much joy in Israel. By an intriguing chain of events, she would marry a righteous Israelite named Boaz, and to them would be born a son named Obed. Obed had a son named Jesse. Jesse had a son named David.

Ruth was to be honored for all time as the great-grandmother of King David, Israel's mightiest king.

And that's not all. Matthew makes a special mention of Ruth as being an ancestress of the greatest man who ever lived, the Lord Jesus Christ.

Stick tight where you ought to be. Be loyal, whether it be to your cause, your country, your spouse, or your children. Don't let the opposition pull you out of place.

Adapted from Ruth 1.

The Power of iPod

Recently, we traveled as a family to visit relatives in another state. We were about an hour into the trip when I heard a commotion in the back seat. I looked into the rear-view mirror and witnessed a most comical sight. Two of our teenage daughters had a single iPod between them and were sharing the earphones. Hannah had an earphone in her right ear, and Shaina had the other in her left ear. The funny sight was this skinny cord connecting the brains of my two girls. It was as close to two people sharing a brain as I have ever seen. Even funnier was what they were doing. No one else in the car could hear what they could hear, yet they were singing at the top of their lungs, or as loud as I would let them, and they were doing it in unison.

I kept watching. It amazed me how much in sync they were, and not just with singing. One moment, they were singing the exact same words in perfect unison; the next, they were laughing; then there was the annoying percussion as they pounded on the seat, again in rhythm with hand and body actions, all in total unity. They entertained themselves for well more than an hour this way. And with more than four hundred songs to choose from, they could have gone on until virtual exhaustion.

These two girls are very different. They have nearly opposite tastes in music, movies, boys, and other such vital things, and yet by the power of iPod they were one. As I watched them, I thought to myself, *If only there was a way to bring individuals, families, and nations into such a harmony. If only there was a way to connect the brains and hearts of all men so they would think as one, feel as one, act as one, be one.*

But there is! The power that connects all men and makes them one in heart, mind, and soul is the power of the Holy Ghost. Across peoples, cultures, languages, and even race, He is always the same, His message is always the same, and He always brings men into unity and harmony with each other and with God. Two people filled with the Spirit of God cannot long remain two in mind and heart. They must become one.

We worship the Father, in the name of the Son, by the power of the Holy Ghost. What is more important today in your schedule than qualifying yourself for His presence?

THING OF NAUGHT

On Friday, the Son of God and Lord of life was judged as evil and not worthy to live. They stripped Him of His clothes and nailed Him to a Cross. He was crucified for our sins. He died for us.

Have you considered how His atoning agony, already incomprehensible, must surely have been intensified by the cruel words of those who stood by His cross? Carefully consider what they said as He hung and suffered there.

The passersby "railed on Him, wagging their heads, and saying, Ah, thou who destroyest the temple, and buildest it in three days, save thyself, and come down from the cross" (Mark 15:29-30).

Can't you just hear the taunt, "If you really were of God and had the power you claimed, you would come down from there."

The chief priests joined in and said, mockingly, "He saved others; let Him save Himself, if He be the Christ, the chosen of God" (Luke 23:35).

It was as if the rulers were saying to all Israel, "See, He's not of God. God would never let such a thing as this happen to a truly righteous man."

Even the soldiers took up the mocking chorus. "If thou be the King of the Jews, save thyself" (Luke 23:37).

And finally, the thief at His side said, "If thou be Christ, save thyself and us" (Luke 23:39).

All seemed to be saying, "You are a liar. If you were all you said you were, this would not be happening to you. Hypocrite! Deceiver!"

Did all of this hurt the Savior? Oh, yes! Through the Psalmist He said, "Reproach hath broken my heart; and I am full of heaviness;

and I looked for some to take pity but there was none: and for comforters but I found none" (Psalms 69:20).

They did not understand. No good man, they assumed, and especially the Son of God, would ever be crucified. They arrogantly judged Him as evil by His circumstance, just as Isaiah said they would.

"Surely He hath borne our griefs and carried our sorrows, yet we did esteem Him stricken, smitten of God and afflicted" (Isaiah 53:4).

They blindly considered Jesus's crucifixion as punishment by God, and so accused Him. What they did not understand was that Jesus the Just was being punished for us, the unjust. His suffering was ours, and His death was for us. God was punishing Him with our stripes. And their caustic words only made it worse.

When it was said, "They shall look on [Him] whom they pierced" (Zechariah 12:10), I wonder, was it only the spear that pierced His heart that day?

Today, the worst of things will happen to the best of people: rebellion of children, ruin, scandal, and divorce. I pray never again will I make their heart's cross heavier by my wagging head and careless words. For I have come to believe that those who spend their time weighting the crosses of others will sooner or later get nailed to one.

Wee Granny

Any whose heart and home have been torn asunder by hate and anger will appreciate just how precious and rare is Zion.

The Lord called his people *Zion* because they were of one heart and one mind and dwelt in righteousness. Zion are a people who are one in the love and doctrine of Christ, enjoying His peace and power. There is no earthly society closer to perfection than Zion. They are the love of heaven on earth.

God and His prophets have been trying to frame Zion for more than six thousand years. But before Zion can be built on our land and into our government, it must be established in our hearts and homes. Will it ever happen?

Many years ago, there lived in Scotland a small but strong woman named Mary Murray. She wasn't even five feet tall. While still young, her beloved husband, James Murdoch, was killed in a mining accident, leaving her with seven children to care for.

Mary went to work, and she worked hard. They lived on oatmeal, potatoes, and salt. As the children grew, they hired out. Eventually, Mary and her family were able to build their own thatched-roof cottage. They had none of the world's wealth, but they knew much love in that humble home.

Then missionaries came and taught the family the gospel of Jesus Christ. Some of the children immigrated to the United States. Finally, in 1856, at the age of seventy-four, Wee Granny Murdoch set out on the six-thousand-mile trek to Zion. For six weeks she endured the hardships of ocean travel, followed by a trip across the country to Iowa City by rail.

Then in late July, Wee Granny began the last leg of the journey to Zion with the Martin Handcart Company. It was late in the season.

And because it was late, they walked to their very limits each day, which eventually became too much for her frail body. At Chimney Rock, Nebraska, on October 2, 1856, Wee Granny Murdoch lay on the prairie, breathing her last.

"Tell John," she said, speaking of her son, "I died with my face toward Zion." And there they buried her beside the trail.

Mary Murray Murdoch died believing she did not make it to Zion. But when Wee Granny set her heart on being one with the Lord and His people, she was already there.

The word *diligent* is used often in scripture. It means to be constant and persistent in our efforts to accomplish something. If you would know the Savior's peace in your heart, in your home, in your community, and in your nation, do as did Wee Granny. Set your face toward Zion and be diligent and determined to the end! It is the only way we will obtain it. Is is worth the journey? It is, I promise!

Lorilee Richardson of South Jordan, Utah, provided the acount and is the great-great-great-granddaughter of Mary Murray Murdoch, "Wee Granny."

Words Matter

Recently, while I was traveling through eastern Idaho and western Wyoming, a thick pall of dense smoke hung in the air for hundreds of miles. It smelled palpably of burned pine. Oddly, though, I never did find the source of the fire. Consider these words of James, the Lord's brother: "The tongue is a little member, and boasteth great things. Behold, how great a forest a little fire kindleth" (James 3:5). As one spark may consume a beautiful forest, one careless word may destroy a life and change the course of men and nations.

A man once had a dream. He found himself flying high in the air. The feeling of power and exhilaration was wonderful. And the view! He could see so far and in so many different directions. It captured the whole of his attention just taking in all that he could now see. Presently, he was startled by something that came flying up past his head. It was a hard, plastic ball a little larger than a softball. Then came another and another. He looked down to see where they came from and was surprised to see a group of people standing together looking up at him. They were talking about him and pointing at him. One threw another ball and it hit him. "Ow," he cried, "that hurts. Stop!" But the people acted as though he could not see them or hear them. They went on pelting him without mercy.

He flew away to escape, but to his dismay, everywhere he went people of all ages pointed and threw those hard balls at him.

"My friends," he thought, "I'll be safe there." And he flew to them. But when they saw him above them, they too pointed and talked in hushed tones. One threw a ball. It hit him in the head. The pain was terrible, so much worse than the others. He cried to them to stop, but they went on as though it was only a harmless sport of no consequence.

Finally, he had enough. He could take no more. Angrily, he flew straight to the ground into their midst. They welcomed him warmly. Strangely, they launched no more balls at him after that.

But after a time, he longed to fly again. Oh, how he missed the power and perspective he had once known. It was the hardest decision he had ever made. Was the power of flight and freedom worth the pain that would surely come? It was, and he lifted off once again, taking his friend with him.

It wasn't long before his friend turned to him. "I see what you mean," he said, tears of pain streaking and etching his face. "I am so sorry I ever threw a ball at you."

The balls would always hurt, but over time the pain became swallowed up in the joy of helping others fly.

Now and ever more, words matter so much! Blessed are those whose mouths are a fountain of virtue and truth. How blessed on the mountains are their feet.

For the New Year

What did Jesus do after his first Christmas? Joseph and Mary were in Egypt for their safety. The angel of the Lord came to Joseph to let him know it was safe to return, and they settled in Nazareth of Galilee (see Matthew 2:22–23). Christmas was over now for the holy family, and the mortal probation of God's Son was underway.

Understand that mortality is indeed a probation (see Alma 12:24). Each of us here was given a body, a mind, and a heart. And we were given the time, the means, and the commandment to improve all three (see Alma 34:33). With the gift of a body, mind, and heart, we are to live life, love God, and love our fellow man. It was the same for Jesus as it is for us, and more so for Him, for "where much is given much is required" (D&C 82:3).

Will the progress be slow? Will perfection take time and patience? It will for us. Even Jesus waited thirty years from that first Christmas until His ministry began (see JST, Matthew 3:26).

Remember that Jesus grew up and "served under His father." Joseph was a carpenter. Thereby, with that kind of work, Jesus not only grew physically, but he "waxed strong" (see JST, Matthew 3:24). Jesus was a physically strong man. My friends, there is indescribable joy in mastering and strengthening the physical body.

Jesus also grew spiritually. Luke records that he "waxed strong in Spirit . . . and the grace of God was upon Him" (Luke 2:40), that he "increased in favor with God" (Luke 2:52). Jesus was close to His Father.

As we study, obey, and pray, it will be the same for us, and it will feel so good.

Luke also says that during His boyhood, Jesus "increased in wisdom," "being filled with wisdom" (Luke 2:52, 40). Wisdom is vision and power. The Savior developed His mind while still a child to an astonishing degree (see John 7:15), becoming wiser than any man in His generation, even Solomon himself (see Luke 11:31). It is for us as it was for Him. The mind must be developed by prayer and by diligent study.

It's also fascinating to know that even in His youth, Jesus "spake not as other men" and "neither could he be taught; for he needed not that any man should teach Him" (JST, Matthew 3:25). The Savior was so far above every man in every way, yet as He increased in favor with God, Jesus also increased in favor with man (see Luke 40:52). In other words, in Jesus's early years, people liked Him. In stark contrast to the hate and crucifixion at the end of His life, He was loved and favored by those who knew Him at the beginning of His life. He loved and was loved, just as I hope it happens with us.

Do as Jesus did after His first Christmas. Grow in mind, body, and spirit. Open your heart, and love God and man.

You know, as we let the Savior in, as we grow as He grew, He takes us from grace to grace, higher and higher in power and perfection of mind, body, and heart—until that perfect day that we are with Him.

Resurrection Morning

Mary Magdalene is a most blessed woman. But you should know that before God exalts, He always brings low.

Sunday morning while it was still dark, Mary came with the other women to complete the anointing of the Lord's body. They found the stone already rolled back and His body gone. Angels greeted them and instructed them to go and tell His disciples that He was risen. But they didn't understand what that meant.

Mary Magdalene ran to tell Peter while the other women went to tell the disciples. Peter and John received that news, and immediately they ran to the tomb to see for themselves. And indeed, He was gone!

The two Apostles left the sepulchre and returned to their homes, but Mary stood outside the tomb weeping, as she had already done for so many hours that weekend. His disappearance from the tomb was one more devastating blow to a heart already broken beyond belief. She had lost Him again! She believed that out of hate and spite, the Jews had stolen His body. Weeping, she stooped down and looked once more into the tomb.

Two angels dressed in white asked her, "Woman, why weepest thou?" (John 20:13).

Her answer reveals her anguish: "Because they have taken away [the body of] my Lord, and I know not where they have laid him" (John 20:13).

At this point, Mary turned around and saw Jesus standing nearby, but she didn't recognize Him.

The Savior comprehended her tears and pain, and He was moved with compassion for her. "Woman," He said, "why weepest thou? whom seekest thou?" (John 20:15).

She thought He was the gardener with authority for the grounds, and she pleaded, "Sir, If thou hast borne him hence, tell me where thou hast laid him, and I will take him away" (John 20:15). And while she was saying this, she turned back and looked once more into the empty tomb.

"Mary" Jesus said (John 20:16).

Mary turned. She recognized Him, and a torrent of light and joy flooded through her soul—as exquisite as had been her grief for a long weekend, so now was the intensity of her joy.

"Rabboni," she cried (John 20:16).

Overcome with emotion, she ran to Him, desiring to hold Him and express with her arms what she felt in her heart. She lost Him once on the cross, and she lost Him again when she thought His body was stolen. Never would she let Him go again!

But understanding her heart, Jesus said to her, "Hold me not; for I have not yet ascended to my Father" (JST, John 20:17). In other words, "Mary, you can't keep me here. I have to leave."

To all of you who love the Lord, Mary was the first to see Him following His resurrection; she wasn't the last. But her reunion with Him reveals something of what it will be like for you who have loved Him and lived your whole lives proving that love.

You will see Him again! Now, live for it!

Jesus and the Prisoners

There is no prison worse than the one we put ourselves in. In ancient Jerusalem, there was a man beside the pool of Bethesda. He was called impotent because he had no power; he couldn't walk; he was helpless. John makes mention of him in the fifth chapter. He was terribly afflicted, and he was scarcely able even to move. He languished in lonely misery beside that pool waiting with many others for the water to stir, hoping that by some miracle he, this time, might be the first to enter the angel's waters and be healed.

It has been thirty-eight years since his sins so entrapped and afflicted him. Can you imagine? Thirty-eight desperate years he has done all he could to free himself of this physical, emotional, and spiritual prison—and to no avail. Where was his hope?

Then one day a stranger entered the porches of Bethesda and walked among the multitude of sick people. Coming to the man, Jesus knew him, and He stopped.

"Wilt thou be made whole?" the Savior asked (John 5:6).

"Sir," the crippled man respectfully replied, "I have no man, when the water is troubled, to put me into the pool: but while I am coming another steppeth down before me" (John 5:7).

"Rise," the Master said, "Take up thy bed and walk." (John 5:8).

And for the first time in almost forty long years, the impotent man stood; he walked, and he was whole. Having no power to come to Jesus, Jesus came to Him. And so He will to all of us.

The Savior has said repeatedly, "Come unto me."

But there are some who just don't know how to come. And there are some who think this journey can be made whenever and however they choose, or that it's a one-time trip.

They are mistaken! The journey to Jesus takes a lifetime and beyond. None of us has any more power to come to Jesus than He gives us, nor can we come any closer to Him than He allows.

Praise be to God! He loves us—all of us. And He wants all of us near Him, in Him. And He will at the appointed time come for each of us, even and especially for those humble prisoners who want so desperately to come and be closer to Him, but they just don't know how.

Be patient and do your best. He's watching, and He will come!

Adapted from John 5:2–9.

Bethlehem Today

Each year the songs and stories of Christmas evoke, at least for me, an image of Bethlehem as a quiet, sleepy, pastoral village surrounded by sheep, illuminated by stars, and watched over by angels. It makes me think of Bethlehem as a place of peace.

So you can imagine my surprise when I learned that today there is a twenty-four-foot concrete wall topped with razor-wire surrounding the city of Bethlehem on three sides. Where Joseph and Mary once entered the city without difficulty, today they couldn't even get in.

According to the December 2007 issue of *National Geographic* magazine, there are guards armed with assault rifles that guard the gate of Bethlehem. Israelis cannot get in, and only a few Palestinians are allowed out.

And where once rumors of miracle babies, John the Baptist, and Jesus once spread throughout that area with great speed, now it can take as long as a month just to get a postcard six miles from Bethlehem on the west bank into Jerusalem.

And where once Bethlehem belonged to the Jews and they were ruled by Rome, now the city belongs primarily to Muslims, and they are ruled by Jews. And tragically, out of Bethlehem have come at least a dozen suicide bombers.

Back then, *Bethlehem* meant "house of bread," and out of it came Jesus, the Bread of Life, the giver of the abundant life. Today in Bethlehem, unemployment runs 50 percent, and the people are desperate and dependent.

Two thousand years ago, the city was so crowded with people from out of town that the inns were full, and Mary and Joseph could find shelter and comfort only in a stable. Now the hotels of Bethlehem are nearly empty; few people spend the night there.

The residents of the city are prisoners, and refugee camps fringe its borders.

And what of that holy stable where the shepherds came in peace and joy to the place where the Christ child was born? That site today resembles a stone fortress. A scant few tourists are escorted in and quickly they depart. Three modern Christian churches presently occupy the Church of the Nativity, and they fight continually for dominance over it. The guards who are placed to guard the church also guard the priests to keep them from attacking each other.

Bethlehem could be called "the" city of Christians, yet today the Christians are fleeing the city. It was once 90 percent Christian. Today it's less than a third, and those numbers are dwindling rapidly.

Ironically, to the Israelis Christians are Palestinian, and to the Palestinians the Christians are foreigners or infidels. Christians in Bethlehem are simply outsiders.

Yes, Bethlehem is Christmas, yet the very holiday itself is celebrated on three different days in Bethlehem. It was here that the Prince of Peace came into the world amid tidings of joy and good will, yet there is no peace. Bethlehem is a city of misery and one of the most contentious places on earth. Joy to the world? Bethlehem is a living testament that the joy of Christmas and the message of Christ are not reaching the world.

Hate is still strong, "and mocks the song of peace on earth, good will to men" ("I Heard the Bells on Christmas Day").

It is vital that we become as children so as to say in June what we sang in December:

I love Thee, Lord Jesus, look down from the sky
And stay by my cradle til morning is nigh.
Be near me, Lord Jesus, I ask Thee to stay
Close by me forever, and love me, I pray.
Bless all the dear children in thy tender care,

And take us to [fit us for] heaven, to live with Thee there.
("Away in a Manger")

Indeed, and with some emotion, let there be peace on earth, and let it begin with me—now!

"All He Needs Is a Coffin"

Andrew May was born February 22, 1871, at Call's Fort, north of Brigham City in Box Elder County, Utah. It was there in June 1894 that Andrew suffered a terrible injury. He was up on a loose haystack. This is Andrew's own account of what happened.

It was about eleven a.m. in the forenoon and Conrad Nelson was running the Jackson fork. The hay was green. A load came up and I called to Nelson to trip it and I thought the fork had gone over me. As I raised up, the long fork tine stuck me in the back and went right through my body. The tine broke my ribs and pushed the bones through my breast.

Hyrum G. Smith (late Patriarch of the Church) was working across the fence and was one of the first to reach me. He helped carry me on a sheet into Brother Wright's house. They sent to Brigham City for Dr. Carrington, who arrived about 5 p.m. He just looked me over, probed the wound, took some blood out of my lungs through my breast and said... "There is no use doing anything for a dead man, all he needs is a wooden overcoat (a coffin). He will not need anything more. I cannot do anything for him...."

The doctor declared that even if Andrew by some miracle did survive, he would be weak and sickly the rest of his life. And with that, the doctor returned to Brigham City without treating him. Andrew continues:

President Lorenzo Snow was in Brigham City and the next morning he heard of my accident . . . and came to our house to see me. He and my father were good friends. He came in, looked me over, and my wife asked him to administer to me. Instead of doing so, he stood by the bedside and asked if I had been anointed. He was told that I had. He then put his hands on my head and gave me a wonderful blessing. The doctor said I was going to die, but President Snow said to me I would not die, but that I would live just as long as life was desirable unto me. He said if I would be faithful to the gospel, I would hold responsible positions in the Church and that I would fill a mission.

The local *Brigham City Bugler* reported, "He seemed to almost immediately revive, and now declares that at the time he heard and felt the pieces of the broken rib reunite. He has practically suffered no pain since from the terrible wound and has been able to sleep comfortably every night since the accident. His recovery has been so steady and rapid as to be a marvel to his friends."

As to serving a mission, Andrew was called to serve as a missionary in New York, where the Church began. He was a bold and courageous missionary.

On June 28, 1908, Andrew was called as bishop of the Rockland Idaho Ward, a position he would hold longer than any other man in that ward—just under seventeen years. His ward members said of him, "Bishop May was a jovial man. He could get a laugh out of most any occurrence, yet he had a tender heart. He was not easily offended. He was like a green sapling, which, when bent to the ground by a rude hand, would spring back to normal once the hold was released."

Andrew May concluded his testimony by saying:

> I have been, and am now Representative in the Idaho Legislature, from Power County, Idaho. President Snow said I would always be active and that I would take pleasure in my work. I have good health, Everything President Snow said has been fulfilled. I have borne this testimony hundreds of times.

And as to the long life promised by President Snow, Andrew May passed away February 6, 1958, just sixteen days short of his eighty-seventh birthday.

Source:
https://www.familysearch.org/tree/person/memories/KWCY-HLL

Story recommended by Aaron Clegg,
https://mail.google.com/mail/u/0/?tab=rm&ogbl#inbox/FMfcgxwKhqddwJVMcfFZWmJtFRVxSJfq

Index

A

A+, earned by student who kept Sabbath, 67–68
Abide
    definition of, 176
    in Christ, 176
Abraham, commanded to sacrifice Isaac, 113–114, 157–158
Adam, partook of forbidden fruit, 105
Adulterous woman, blessed by Jesus, 56–57
Ahaz
    bargaining for his nation's safety, 11
    refusing to ask for a sign, 11
    told by Isaiah not to fear enemy kings, 11
Airplane, leaving iPad on, 208–209
Alma the Younger, repentance of, 187
Ames, Ira, dream of about Isaiah 11, 73–74
Apostles, as martyrs, 144
Arabella, experience at Hole-in-the-Rock, 69–71
Artificial heart, young man received, 24
Assyrian, army defeated by Hezekiah, 93–94
Atonement
    crucifixion as part of, 131
    of Jesus, 16–22

B

Babysitter, comforted by the Holy Ghost, 79–80
Ballard, Melvin J., vision of Savior to, 188
Balloon, little girl losing, 83
Barnes, Lorenzo Dow
    Joseph Smith's tribute to, 141
    monument to, 141
    service of, 140–141
Bartimaeus, experience with Jesus, 169–170
Bethesda, man at pool of, 226
Bethlehem, condition of modern-day, 228–230
Blizzard, experience of driving through, 175–176
Boaz, marriage of to Ruth, 213
Book, in parable of the map, 120–122
Bread of Life, Jesus as, 65–66, 81–82
Bread
    as staff of life, 66

given to Elijah by widow, 40–42
used to feed the five thousand, 65
Breathing, miracle of, 197
Burial, of woman by side of trail, 95–96

C

Caleb, sent as spy to land of Canaan, 101–102
Cell phone, as metaphor for prayer, 127–128
Cheer, expressed by Jesus, 26
Chimney Rock, Wee Granny's death at, 219
Christmas
    gift of keyboard, 192–193
    reminder that God can do the impossible, 12
Climbing, Tetons, 97–98
Coffin, carried to Salt Lake Valley, 7
Comforter, the Holy Ghost, 79–80
Commandments
    dying grandfather's message to keep, 2
    show love of Jesus by keeping, 4
Concert, sleeping at, 171–172
Congress, service of Thomas Jefferson in, 179–180
Conrad, Susan, marriage of to Lorenzo Dow Barnes, 140
Constitutional Convention, 133
Conversion, of Saul, 150–151
Cross-country skiing, lost while, 89–90
Crucifixion, of Jesus, 15

D

Daniel, 38–39
    condemned to death, 38
    interpretation of Nebuchadnezzar's dream, 39, 123–124
    refused to stop praying, 39
    thrown into lion's den, 38
David
    and Goliath, 43–45
    born in Ruth's lineage, 213
Decisions, affect rest of life, 29–30
Diligent, definition of, 218
Dirt, spread on road in Philadelphia, 107
Disciples, appearance of resurrected Jesus to, 188–189
Dog
    chasing horses, 167
    injured by pack of ranch dogs, 19
    killed chasing cars, 19–20
Doubts, appropriate way to handle, 73–74
Dream
    of balls being thrown at man, 220–221
    of Joseph Smith, 194–195
    of King Nebuchadnezzar, interpreted by Daniel, 39, 123–124
Driver, of garbage truck, 111–112

E

Earth, interaction with sun, 197
Egypt, flight of Holy Family to, 222
Elderly man, who had lost his way, 135–137
Eli, prophecy to Hannah of a child, 177–178
Elijah, and the widow of Zarephath, 40–42
Elisha, assuring king during Syrian attack, 109–110
Endurance, 206–207

Eve, partook of forbidden fruit, 105
Example, importance of, 165–166

F

Faith
    precedes the miracle, 39
    skiing used as metaphor for, 89–90
Families, forever, 1–2
Father
    honor, 184
    responsibilities of, 138–139
    will of, Jesus did, 21–23
Fatherhood, of God, 34–35
Fear, no reason to, 167–168
Feet, massaging dying grandfather's, 1
First Vision, 187
Fish, used to feed the five thousand, 65
Five thousand, Jesus feeding, 81
Flight attendant, running to get iPad on other plane, 208–209
Fuel, running out of on freeway, 46–47

G

Garbage truck, driver of, 111–112
Garden of Eden, Adam and Eve cast out of, 105
Gas, running out of on freeway, 46–47
Gethsemane
    greatest expression of love, 4
    Jesus's pain in, 131
Girl, running away, 54–55
Give up, those who don't, 207
Gnat, on pillow, 185
God
    fatherhood of, 34–35
    knows your name, 197
    love of for us, 3
    power of, 197
    unchangeable nature of, 37
Golgotha, greatest expression of love, 4
Goliath, slain by David, 43–45
Grandfather, dying message to family, 1–2
Granger High School, seminary class at, 115–116
Granny, Wee, 218–219
Grant, Caroline, death of, 6
Grant, Jedediah Morgan
    carried wife's coffin to Salt Lake Valley, 6–7
    death of wife and baby, 6
    finding baby's grave empty, 7
    visit to spirit world, 7
Gratitude, importance of, 192–193
Grave, finding great-grandmother's, 58–59
Great-grandmother, finding grave of, 58–59

H

Hair, little boy styling own, 165–166
Haircut, little boy wanted one like his father, 13
Hall family, prayer that set example, 75–76
Hannah, prayer of for a child, 177–178
Heart failure, of young man, 24–25
Heart transplant, young man received, 24–25
Heart, miracle of, 196–197
Heaven, lay up treasures in, 31
Hey Diddle Diddle, 159
Hezekiah, deliverance of from Assyrians, 93–94, 190–191
Hole-in-the-Rock, traversed by Smiths, 69–71
Holy Ghost
    as teacher of truth, 160

as the Comforter, 79–80
comforting frightened babysitter, 79–80
connects all men, 215
Horses, being chased by dog, 167
Humbling, of Nebuchadnezzar, 123–124

I

Independence Hall, dirt spread on street in front of, 107
iPad, leaving on plane, 208–209
iPod, bringing girls together in back seat, 214
Isaac, command to Abraham to sacrifice, 113–114, 157–158
Isaiah
    as a martyr, 144
    assures Hezekiah in battle, 93–94
    description of Savior, 117
    message of to Ahaz not to fear enemy kings, 11
    prophesies of Jesus's birth, 11–12
Isaiah 11, dream of Ira Ames about, 73–74

J

Jacob's well, Jesus at, 87–88
Jairus, raising of daughter from the dead, 85–86
James
    as a martyr, 144
    upset at treatment of Jesus, 200
Jefferson, Thomas
    death of child, 179
    destiny of, 179–180
Jesus
    and rich young man, 99–100
    and the woman at the well, 87–88
    as Bread of Life, 65–66, 81–82
    born in lineage of Ruth, 213
    command of to help others, 129–130
    commanding disciples to feed His sheep, 5
    commanding disciples to love one another, 3–4
    commandment of to abide in Him, 176
    crucifixion of, 15, 216–217
    defending woman taken in adultery, 56–57
    defense of by James and John, 200
    described by Isaiah, 117
    did not give up, 207
    evidence of His cheer, 26
    examples of not judging others, 198–199
    experiences of mortality, 117–119
    experiences of with prayer, 161–162
    feeding the five thousand, 65–66, 81
    flight to Egypt, 222
    found in temple at age of twelve, 21
    greatest pioneer of all, 16
    healing Bartimaeus, 169–170
    healing man at Pool of Bethesda, 226
    healing of nobleman's son, 146–147
    in temple at age of twelve, 183
    interactions with mother, 52–53
    little girl running away to, 54–55
    pain of during crucifixion, 131

pain of in Gethsemane, 131
raising daughter of Jairus from the dead, 85–86
raising son of widow of Nain, 77–78
resurrection of, 15–16, 224–225
temptations of, 210–211
those who have seen in vision, 187–189
turning water to wine, 52–53
visit to home of Martha and Mary, 9–10
visit to American continent, 21
vows to do will of the Father, 21–23
youth of, 223

Johann, battle with cancer, 50–51
Johansen, John, experience of in thunderstorm, 163–164
John, upset at treatment of Jesus, 200
Jonah
    angry with God over dead plant, 35
    powerful call to repentance in Nineveh, 34–35
Joshua
    message to Israel about serving the Lord, 17
    sent as spy to land of Canaan, 101–102

K

Keyboard, Christmas gift of, 192–193
King Darius, condemned Daniel to death, 38
King Nebuchadnezzar, dream of interpreted by Daniel, 39

L

Least of these, Jesus's command to help, 129–130
Life, show love by laying down for another, 4
Lincoln, Abraham, proposal of marriage to Mary Owens, 152–153
Lions, Daniel thrown into den of, 38
Lorenzo Dow Barnes, marriage of, 140
Love
    always involves sacrifice, 4
    definition of, 3
    forever, 1
    highest expression of, 4
    memories of, 202–203
    of God, 3

M

Magdalene, Mary, at resurrection of Jesus, 15–16, 224–225
Malaria, afflicting family of Stillman Pond, 173–174
Map, parable of, 120–122
Marriage, proposal of by Abraham Lincoln, 152–153
Martha, busily preparing to feed Jesus, 9
Martin Handcart Company, Wee Granny's trek with, 218–219
Martyrs, examples of, 144
Mary Magdalene, at resurrection of Jesus, 15–16, 224–225
Mary, sits at feet of Jesus, 9
Massage, of dying grandfather's feet, 1
Maxwell, Neal A., phone call to cancer victim, 50–51
May, Andrew, injury and healing of, 231–232
Memorial Day, purpose of, 144
Miracle, preceded by faith, 39
Mission, of Lorenzo Dow Barnes, 140
Missionaries

in thunderstorm, 163–164
Lord protects, 163–164
teaching gang members, 167–168
Mob, threatening Joseph F. Smith, 48–49
Mocking, destructive effects of, 216–217
Money
son who gave to grandparents, 32
used to help others, 204–205
Mortality, as probation, 222–223
Mortgage, son who paid for parents, 31–32
Moses
given mission by the Lord, 185
sent spies to land of Canaan, 101–102
vision of worth of man, 185–186
Mother
honor, 183–184
of Jesus, 52–53
Motherhood, importance of, 177–178
Murdoch, Mary Murray, trek to Zion, 218–219
Murdock, John, account of vision of the Savior, 187
Music, power of, 116

N

Nain, widow of, 77–78
Name, God knows your, 197
Naomi, loyalty of Ruth to, 212
Nebuchadnezzar
Daniel refused to eat foods of, 38–39
dream of, 123–124
Nelson, Russell M., quote on entertainment, 116
Nineveh, repentance of people in, 34–35
Nobleman, son of healed by Jesus, 146–147
Norris Geyser Basin, 36

O

Obedience
and rich young man, 99–100
demonstrated by widow of Zarephath, 40–42
importance of, 99–100
Old Faithful, 36–37
Old Mustard, pickup truck, 125–126
Orpah, story of, 212
Owens, Mary, proposal of marriage to by Abraham Lincoln, 152–153

P

Pacing, importance of, 206–207
Pain
of body, 131
of Jesus, 131–132
of spirit, 131
Parents, love between, 202–203
Patience
definition of, 201
importance of, 201
Paul
conversion of, 150–151
former life as Saul, 150–151
Peter, as a martyr, 144
Pharisee, behavior of, 60–61
Philadelphia, dirt spread on road in, 107
Piano, wanting to buy for student, 204–205
Pica, definition of, 148
Pickup truck, Old Mustard, 125–126
Pioneer, Jesus the greatest of all, 16
Pioneer trail, road trip along, 154–156

Plant, Jonah's experience with God about, 35
Plod, definition of, 206
Pond, Abigail A., death of, 173
Pond, Harriet M., death of, 173
Pond, Laura Jane, death of, 173
Pond, Lyman, death of, 173
Pond, Marie, death of, 174
Pond, Stillman
    death of children, 173–174
    suffering of, 173–174
Pool of Bethesda, Jesus healing man at, 226
Porcupine, class project to follow, 181–182
Pray, commandment to, 162
Prayer
    answer to, 28
    experiences of Jesus with, 161–162
    family, example set by, 75–76
    power of, 25, 127–128
    regarding truth of gospel, 27–28
Praying, for others, power of, 25
President, of the United States, 133–134
Promised land, ability to reach, 102
Proposal, of marriage by Abraham Lincoln, 152–153
Publican, behavior of, 60–61

Q

Questions, appropriate way to handle, 73–74

R

Red Flake, in Tetons, 97–98
Redding, Alma, experience of in thunderstorm, 163–164
Repentance, of Alma the Younger, 187
Resurrection, 15–16
Revelation, comes during stillness, 107–108
Rice, sweet-and-sour, prepared for wife, 103–104
Road trip, along pioneer trail, 154–156
Ruth
    ancestor of Jesus, 213
    marriage of to Boaz, 213
    story of, 212–213

S

Sacrifice, a quality of perfect love, 4
Samaritan woman, at Jacob's well, 87-88
Samuel, born to Hannah after prophecy, 177–178
Saul
    conversion of, 150–151
    sending David to meet Goliath, 44
School of the Prophets, vision of Savior to, 187
Seminary student, playing guitar in class, 115–116
Sheep, feed my, command of Jesus, 5
Sin, doing something good at the wrong time, 211
Skiing
    lost while, 89–90
    metaphor for faith, 89–90
Smiling, Jesus, 26
Smith, Arabella, experience at Hole-in-the-Rock, 69–71
Smith, Hyrum, as a martyr, 145
Smith, Jesse Nathaniel, reaction of burial of woman, 95–96
Smith, Joseph F., standing up to drunken mob, 48–49
Smith, Joseph Stanford, experience at Hole-in-the-Rock, 69–71
Smith, Joseph

as a martyr, 145
comments about Lorenzo Dow Barnes, 141
dream of in stormy water, 194–195
First Vision of, 187

Snow, Lorenzo
healing of Andrew May, 232
prayer of to gain testimony, 27–28

Soap, woman who ate during pregnancy, 148–149

Son, of widow of Nain, raised from the dead, 77–78

Song, about losing our way, 135–137

Sons of thunder, 200

Spies, sent to land of Canaan, 101–102

Spiritual fuel, 46–47

Steamboat Geyser, doesn't erupt faithfully, 36–37

Stockings, name of Collie dog, 19

Stolen, stop sign, 17–18

Stop sign, stolen, 17–18

Storm, on waters, Joseph Smith dream about, 194–195

Sun, interaction with sun, 197

Sweet-and-sour rice, prepared for wife, 103–104

Swings
metaphor for moving on in life, 72
pushing children on, 72

T

Temptation, 210–211
Tetons, climbing, 97–98
Thanksgiving, importance of, 192–193
They that be with us, 109–110
Tire repairman, experience with, 62–64
Tires, blowout of on truck, 62–64
Treasures, lay up in heaven, 31
Tree of life, 105–106
Truck
Old Mustard, 125–126
tire blowout on, 62–64
Truth
definition of, 159–160
validated by Holy Ghost, 160
Tumbleweeds, as metaphor for losing way, 142–143
Typing, learning to as an adult, 29–30

U

United States President, duties of, 133–134

V

Vision, of people in stadium praying, 25

W

Wee Granny, 218–219
Weight-lifting, rescue of son while, 91–92
Well, Jesus and Samaritan woman at, 87–88
Widow of Nain, 77–78
Widow of Zarephath, 40–42
Will, of Father, Jesus did, 21–23
Woman
buried by side of trail, 95–96
taken in adultery, 56–57
Woodruff, Wilford, erection of monument to Lorenzo Dow Barnes, 141
Words, damage of careless, 220–221

Z

Zarephath, widow of, 40–42
Zion, definition of, 218